The Congressional Research Service (CRS) works exclusively for the United States Congress, providing policy and legal analysis to committees and Members of both the House and Senate, regardless of party affiliation. As a legislative branch agency within the Library of Congress, CRS has been a valued and respected resource on Capitol Hill for more than a century.

CRS is well-known for analysis that is authoritative, confidential, objective and nonpartisan. Its highest priority is to ensure that Congress has 24/7 access to the nation's best thinking.

You, too, can be among the first to receive CRS research, joining the ranks of U.S. and foreign government agencies, universities, lobbyists, and others who have, de facto, retained the Congressional Research Service as their in-house think-tank.

CRS issues an average of approximately 50 research reports weekly on topics of current legislative interest, ranging alphabetically from Abortion to Zimbabwe. As a subscriber, you have access to our collection of more than 70,000 of these reports.

CONGRESSIONAL RESEARCH REPORT

VOL. XXXIII No. 4   APRIL 2016

DESCRIPTION OF CONTENTS

This monthly report contains descriptions of research performed by the U.S. Congress' Congressional Research Service (CRS) during the past month.

Descriptions are arranged alphabetically by broad topics ranging from "Abortion" to "Women's Issues." Following each description is an order number.

AGRICULTURE

COUNTRY-OF-ORIGIN LABELING FOR FOODS AND THE WTO TRADE DISPUTE ON MEAT LABELING, by Joel L. Greene, Analyst in Agricultural Policy. 62 pages. Updated March 8, 2016. Since the final rule to implement country-of-origin labeling (COOL) took effect in March 2009, most retail food stores have been required to inform consumers about the country of origin of fresh fruits and vegetables, fish, shellfish, peanuts, pecans, macadamia nuts, ginseng, and ground and muscle cuts of beef, pork, lamb, chicken, and goat. The rules are required by the 2002 farm bill (P.L. 107-171) as amended by the 2008 farm bill (P.L. 110-246). Other U.S. laws have required such labeling, but only for imported food products already pre-packaged for consumers. Canada and Mexico challenged U.S. COOL in the World Trade Organization (WTO), arguing that COOL has a trade-distorting impact by reducing the value and number of cattle and hogs shipped to the U.S. market, thus violating WTO trade commitments. In November 2011, the WTO dispute settlement (DS) panel found that COOL treats imported livestock less favorably than U.S. livestock, and does not meet its objective to provide complete information to consumers on the origin of meat products. In March 2012, the United States appealed the WTO ruling. In June 2012 the WTO's Appellate Body (AB) upheld the DS panel's finding that COOL treats imported livestock less favorably

than domestic livestock. But the AB reversed the finding that COOL does not fulfill its legitimate objective to provide consumers with information on origin. The United States welcomed the AB's affirmation of the right to adopt labeling requirements to inform consumers on the origin of their meat. Participants in the U.S. livestock sector had mixed reactions, reflecting the ongoing heated debate on COOL. Bills: P.L. 107-171, P.L. 110-246, H.R. 2393, S. 1844, H.R. 22, P.L. 109-97, P.L. 113-235, H.R. 2642. Order No. RS22955.

EMERGENCY ASSISTANCE FOR AGRICULTURAL LAND REHABILITATION, by Megan Stubbs, Specialist in Agricultural Conservation and Natural Resources Policy. 15 pages. Updated March 10, 2016. This report describes these emergency agricultural land assistance programs. It presents background on the programs-purpose, activities, authority, eligibility requirements, and authorized program funding levels, as well as current congressional issues. Order No. R42854.

NUTRIENTS IN AGRICULTURAL PRODUCTION: A WATER QUALITY OVERVIEW, by Megan Stubbs, Specialist in Agricultural Conservation and Natural Resources Policy. 29 pages. Updated February 29, 2016. This report discusses the types and sources of nutrient pollution from agricultural production; possible environmental effects of nutrient pollution; examples of current control measures; the federal response to excess nutrients, including regulatory and incentive-based programs; and future considerations for nutrient management policy at the federal level. Order No. R43919.

Congressional Research Report is published monthly by Penny Hill Press, 301-253-0881; fax 301- 253-0721; e-mail Books@pennyhill.com
Visit www.PennyHill.com for a full list of Topics and a list of over 70,000 reports.

BUDGET

CONSUMER OPERATED AND ORIENTED PLAN (CO-OP) PROGRAM: FREQUENTLY ASKED QUESTIONS, by Annie L. Mach, Analyst in Health Care Financing; Grant A. Driessen, Analyst in Public Finance. 16 pages. March 11, 2016. The Consumer Operated and Oriented Plan (CO-OP) program was included in the Patient Protection and Affordable Care Act (ACA; P.L. 111-148) in an effort to increase the competitiveness of state health insurance markets and improve choice. Under the program, the Centers for Medicare & Medicaid Services (CMS) uses appropriated funds to award low-interest loans to organizations applying to become CO-OPs-nonprofit, member-run health insurance issuers that sell health insurance in the state(s) in which they are licensed. Order No. R44414.

CONGRESS AND THE BUDGET: 2016 ACTIONS AND EVENTS, by Grant A. Driessen, Analyst in Public Finance; Megan S. Lynch, Specialist on Congress and the Legislative Process. 12 pages. Updated March 23, 2016. Since the budget process will vary significantly each year, it is better understood not as a definite set of actions that must occur annually, but instead as an array of opportunities for affecting the federal budget. This report seeks to assist in (1) anticipating what budget-related actions might occur within the upcoming year, and (2) staying abreast of budget actions that occur this year. It provides a general description of the recurrent types of budgetary actions, and reflects on current events that unfold in each category during 2016. In addition, it includes information on certain events that may affect Congress's work on the budget, such as the President's budget request and the Congressional Budget Office's budget and economic outlook. The most-recent budget actions will be noted at the beginning of the report. Order No. R44347.

CYBERSECURITY: CRITICAL INFRASTRUCTURE AUTHORITATIVE REPORTS AND RESOURCES, by Rita Tehan, Information Research Specialist. 31 pages. March 9, 2016. This report serves as a starting point for congressional staff assigned to cover cybersecurity issues as they relate to critical infrastructure. Much is written about protecting U.S. critical infrastructure, and this CRS report directs the reader to authoritative sources that address many of the most prominent issues. The annotated descriptions of these sources are listed in reverse chronological order with an emphasis on material published in the past several years. The report includes resources and studies from government agencies (federal, state, local, and international), think tanks, academic institutions, news organizations, and other sources. Order No. R44410.

FY2017 APPROPRIATIONS FOR THE DEPARTMENT OF JUSTICE, by Nathan James, Analyst in Crime Policy. 15 pages. March 23, 2016. For FY2016, Congress provided a total of $29.090 billion for DOJ. The Administration proposes a 2.8% increase in DOJ's funding for FY2017 ($29.910 billion). The Administration's request includes $2.789 billion for the U.S. Marshals, $9.502 billion for the FBI, $2.103 billion for the DEA, $1.306 billion for the ATF, $7.302 billion for the BOP, and $2.361 billion for grant programs. Order No. R44424.

FY2017 APPROPRIATIONS FOR THE DEPARTMENT OF JUSTICE GRANT PROGRAMS, by Nathan James, Analyst in Crime Policy. 14 pages. March 23, 2016. For FY2017, the Administration requests a total of $2.361 billion for these five accounts. This includes $489 million for the Office on Violence Against Women (which includes a proposed $326 million transfer from the Crime Victims Fund); $154 million for Research, Evaluation, and Statistics; $1.098 billion for State and Local Law Enforcement Assistance; $334.4 million for Juvenile Justice Programs; and $286 million for

Community Oriented Policing Services. The Administration's request for all of these accounts, with the exception of State and Local Law Enforcement Assistance, is greater than the FY2016 appropriation. Order No. R44430.

MILITARY FUNERAL HONORS FOR VETERANS, by Scott D. Szymendera, Analyst in Disability Policy. 11 pages. March 9, 2016. Eligible veterans are entitled to receive certain military honors at their funerals. In general, these honors are provided by the Department of Defense (DOD) to eligible veterans who are interred or inurned at Department of Veterans Affairs (VA) national cemeteries, state veterans cemeteries, and private cemeteries. There is no cost to the family of a veteran for military honors. Order No. R44426.

NONPROFIT CHALLENGES TO THE CONTRACEPTIVE COVERAGE REQUIREMENT: THE MEANING OF SUBSTANTIAL BURDENS ON RELIGIOUS EXERCISE UNDER THE RELIGIOUS FREEDOM RESTORATION ACT, by Cynthia Brown, Legislative Attorney. 21 pages. March 21, 2016. This report examines the current parameters on governmental restrictions on religious exercise. It discusses the history of federal protection offered under the Free Exercise Clause of the First Amendment and RFRA, and notes parallel protections available at the state level. It analyzes the current interpretations of RFRA as applied to the contraceptive coverage requirement of the ACA, including discussion of Hobby Lobby and a review of the lower courts' interpretations of the nonprofit challenges. Finally, the report highlights a range of issue areas of interest to Congress that may be affected by the Court's interpretation of RFRA. Order No. R44422.

SBA DISASTER LOAN PROGRAM: FREQUENTLY ASKED QUESTIONS, by Bruce R. Lindsay, Analyst in American National Government; William L. Painter, Analyst in

Emergency Management and Homeland Security Policy; Francis X. McCarthy, Analyst in Emergency Management Policy. 15 pages. March 9, 2016. This report responds to frequently asked questions about the Small Business Administration (SBA) Disaster Loan Program. The SBA Disaster Loan Program provides direct loans to help businesses, nonprofit organizations, homeowners, and renters repair or replace property damaged or destroyed in a federally declared disaster. The program is also designed to help small agricultural cooperatives recover from economic injury resulting from a disaster. SBA disaster loans include (1) Home and Personal Property Disaster Loans, (2) Business Physical Disaster Loans, and (3) Economic Injury Disaster Loans (EIDL). Most direct disaster loans (approximately 80%) are awarded to individuals and households rather than small businesses. The program generally offers low-interest disaster loans at a fixed rate with loan maturities of up to 30 years. Order No. R44412.

THE FEDERAL BUDGET: OVERVIEW AND ISSUES FOR FY2017 AND BEYOND, by Grant A. Driessen, Analyst in Public Finance; Megan S. Lynch, Specialist on Congress and the Legislative Process. 24 pages. March 24, 2016. This report summarizes issues surrounding the federal budget and discusses policy changes relevant to the budget framework for FY2017. It also discusses the major policy proposals included in the President's FY2017 budget and, when available, the House and Senate budget resolutions. Finally, this report addresses major short- and long-term fiscal challenges facing the federal government. Order No. R44428.

SBA DISASTER LOAN PROGRAM: FREQUENTLY ASKED QUESTIONS, by Bruce R. Lindsay, Analyst in American National Government; William L. Painter, Analyst in Emergency Management and Homeland Security Policy; Francis X. McCarthy, Analyst in Emergency Management Policy. 15 pages. March 9, 2016. This report responds to frequently asked questions about the Small Business Administration (SBA) Disaster Loan Program. The SBA Disaster Loan Program provides direct loans to help businesses, nonprofit organizations, homeowners, and renters repair or replace property damaged or destroyed in a federally declared disaster. The program is also designed to help small agricultural cooperatives recover from economic injury resulting from a disaster. SBA disaster loans include (1) Home and Personal Property Disaster Loans, (2) Business Physical Disaster Loans, and (3) Economic Injury Disaster Loans (EIDL). Most direct disaster loans (approximately 80%) are awarded to individuals and households rather than small businesses. The program generally offers low-interest disaster loans at a fixed rate with loan maturities of up to 30 years. Order No. R44412.

DEPARTMENT OF HOUSING AND URBAN DEVELOPMENT (HUD): FUNDING TRENDS SINCE FY2002, by Maggie McCarty, Specialist in Housing Policy. 19 pages. Updated March 17, 2016. This report explores the trends in HUD's funding since FY2002. It begins with an explanation of the key budget concepts necessary to understand those trends. It concludes with a discussion of factors that may influence HUD's budget going forward. Order No. R42542.

ENCRYPTION: SELECTED LEGAL ISSUES, by Richard M. Thompson II, Legislative Attorney; Chris Jaikaran, Analyst in Cybersecurity Policy. 32 pages. March 3, 2016. This report first provides background to the ongoing encryption debate, including a primer on encryption basics and an overview of Apple, Google, and Facebook's new encryption policies. Next, it will provide an overview of the Fifth Amendment right to be free from self-incrimination; survey the limited case law concerning the compelled disclosure of encrypted data; and apply this case law to help determine if and when the government may require such disclosures. The next section of the report will provide background on the All Writs Act; explore

both Supreme Court and lower court case law, including a discussion of United States v. New York Tel. Co.; and apply this case law to the San Bernardino case and potential future requests by the government to access a locked device. Bills: H.R. 726, H.R. 2233, H.R. 4651, S. 135, S. 2604. Order No. R44407.

OVERVIEW OF FY2017 APPROPRIATIONS FOR COMMERCE, JUSTICE, SCIENCE, AND RELATED AGENCIES (CJS), by Nathan James, Analyst in Crime Policy.
21 pages. March 7, 2016. This report tracks and describes actions taken by the Administration and Congress to provide FY2017 appropriations for the Commerce, Justice, Science, and Related Agencies (CJS) accounts. It also provides an overview of FY2016 appropriations for agencies and bureaus funded as part of annual CJS appropriations. Order No. R44409.

SELECTED AGENCY BUDGET JUSTIFICATIONS FOR FY2017, by Justin Murray, Information Research Specialist. 7 pages. Updated March 8, 2016. This report provides a convenient listing of online FY2017 agency budget justification submissions for all 15 executive branch departments and 9 selected independent agencies. In most cases, budget justifications contain more detailed descriptions of the proposals and programs that are provided in the President's budget submissions. This report will be updated to reflect the current budget justifications submissions for the forthcoming fiscal year. Order No. R43470.

TRANSPORTATION SPENDING UNDER AN EARMARK BAN, by Robert S. Kirk and William J. Mallett, Specialists in Transportation Policy; David Randall Peterman, Analyst in Transportation Policy. 14 pages. March 17, 2016. Proposals in both the House and the Senate to ban earmarks may lead to changes in the way transportation funding decisions are made. This report explains what earmarks are and discusses their use in surface transportation finance. It then considers how federal highway, transit, and aviation funding might be distributed if such a ban goes into effect, and how members of Congress might influence the distribution. Order No. R41554

BUSINESS

FOREIGN CORRUPT PRACTICES ACT (FCPA): CONGRESSIONAL INTEREST AND EXECUTIVE ENFORCEMENT, by Michael V. Seitzinger, Legislative Attorney. 11 pages. Updated March 15, 2016. During the mid-1970s investigations and administrative and legal actions against numerous domestic corporations revealed that the practice of making questionable or illegal payments by United States corporations to foreign government officials existed to some extent within the American business community. The legal and regulatory mechanisms for dealing with these payments had involved actions by the Securities and Exchange Commission (SEC) against public corporations for concealing from required public disclosure substantial payments made by the firm, including to foreign government officials. There was also the potential for an antitrust action for restraints of trade or fraud prosecutions by the Department of Justice (DOJ). Government officials and administrators contended that more direct prohibitions on foreign bribery and more detailed requirements concerning corporate recordkeeping and accountability were needed to deal effectively with the problem. The revelations of slush funds and secret payments by American corporations were stated to have affected adversely American foreign policy, damaged abroad the image of American democracy, and impaired public confidence in the financial integrity of American corporations. Bills: H.R. 616, H.R. 5366, H.R. 5837, H.R. 2152, H.R. 3531, H.R. 3588, H.R. 4178. Order No. R41466.

SMALL BUSINESS ADMINISTRATION AND JOB CREATION, by Robert Jay Dilger, Senior Specialist in American National Government. 22 pages. Updated March 8, 2016. This report examines the economic research on net job creation to identify the types of businesses that appear to create the most jobs. That research suggests that business startups play an important role in job creation, but have a more limited effect on net job creation over time because fewer than half of all startups are still in business after five years. However, the influence of small business startups on net job creation varies by firm size. Startups with fewer than 20 employees tend to have a negligible effect on net job creation over time whereas startups with 20-499 employees tend to have a positive employment effect, as do surviving younger businesses of all sizes (in operation for one year to five years). This report then examines the possible implications this research might have for Congress and the SBA. For example, the SBA provides assistance to all qualifying businesses that meet its size standards. About 97% of all businesses currently meet the SBA's eligibility criteria. Given congressional interest in job creation, this report examines the potential consequences of targeting small business assistance to a narrower group, small businesses that are the most likely to create and retain the most jobs. This report also examines the arguments for providing federal assistance to small businesses, noting that policy makers often view job creation as a justification for such assistance whereas economists argue that over the long term federal assistance to small businesses is likely to reallocate jobs within the economy, not increase them. Nonetheless, most economists support federal assistance to small businesses for other purposes, such as a means to correct a perceived market failure related to the disadvantages small businesses experience when attempting to access capital and credit. Order No. R41523.

SMALL BUSINESS: ACCESS TO CAPITAL AND JOB CREATION, by Robert Jay Dilger, Senior Specialist in American National

Government. 33 pages. Updated March 1, 2016. The U.S. Small Business Administration (SBA) administers several programs to support small businesses, including loan guaranty and venture capital programs to enhance small business access to capital; contracting programs to increase small business opportunities in federal contracting; direct loan programs for businesses, homeowners, and renters to assist their recovery from natural disasters; and small business management and technical assistance training programs to assist business formation and expansion. Congressional interest in these programs has increased in recent years, primarily because assisting small business is viewed as a means to enhance economic growth. Bills: H.R. 5851, H.R. 2499, H.R. 3584, H.R. 3007, H.R. 5835, H.R. 2451, H.R. 35854, S. 1828. Order No. R40985.

STATE SMALL BUSINESS CREDIT INITIATIVE: IMPLEMENTATION AND FUNDING ISSUES, by Robert Jay Dilger, Senior Specialist in American National Government. 43 pages. Updated March 17, 2016. This report examines the SSBCI and its implementation, including Treasury's response to initial program audits conducted by the U.S. Government Accountability Office (GAO) and Treasury's Office of Inspector General (OIG). These initial audits suggest that SSBCI participants are generally complying with the statute's requirements but that some compliance problems exist. They also indicate that Treasury's oversight of the program could be improved and that performance measures are needed to assess the program's efficacy. Bills: H.R. 4556, H.R. 5297, H.R. 5302, H.R. 5297, H.R. 5486, S. 2285. Order No. R42581.

THE SMALL BUSINESS LENDING FUND, by Robert Jay Dilger, Senior Specialist in American National Government. 39 pages. Updated March 10, 2016. This report focuses on the SBLF. It opens with a discussion of the supply and demand for small business loans. The

SBLF's advocates claimed the SBLF was needed to enhance the supply of small business loans. The report then examines other arguments presented both for and against the program. Advocates argued that the SBLF would increase lending to small businesses and, in turn, create jobs. Opponents contended that the SBLF could lose money, lacked sufficient oversight provisions, did not require lenders to increase their lending to small businesses, could serve as a vehicle for Troubled Asset Relief Program (TARP) recipients to effectively refinance their TARP loans on more favorable terms with little or no resulting benefit for small businesses, and could encourage a failing lender to make even riskier loans to avoid higher dividend payments.

The report concludes with an examination of the program's implementation and a discussion of bills introduced during the 112th and 113th Congresses to amend the SBLF. For example, during the 112th Congress, S. 681, the Greater Accountability in the Lending Fund Act of 2011, would have limited the program's authority to 15 years from enactment and prohibited TARP recipients from participating in the program. H.R. 2807, the Small Business Leg-Up Act of 2011, would have transferred any unobligated and repaid funds from the SBLF to the Community Development Financial Institutions Fund "to increase the availability of credit for small businesses. "H.R. 3147, the Small Business Lending Extension Act, would have extended the Treasury Department's investment authority from one year to two years. During the 113th Congress, H.R. 2474, the Community Lending and Small Business Jobs Act of 2013, would have transferred any unobligated and repaid funds from the SBLF to the Community Development Financial Institutions Fund. Bills: H.R. 2807, H.R. 3147, H.R. 2474, H.R. 2807, H.R. 3147, H.R. 5297, H.R. 1387, S. 681. Order No. R42045.

CHILDREN

INDIVIDUAL TAXPAYER IDENTIFICATION NUMBER (ITIN)

FILERS AND THE CHILD TAX CREDIT: OVERVIEW AND LEGISLATION, by Margot L. Crandall-Hollick, Analyst in Public Finance; Molly F. Sherlock, Coordinator of Division Research and Specialist. 8 pages. March 22, 2016. The child tax credit was created by the Taxpayer Relief Act of 1997 (P.L. 105-34) to help ease the financial burden on families when they have children. The credit offsets a taxpayer's federal income tax liability. It also includes a refundable portion, known as the additional child tax credit (ACTC). The ACTC is available to taxpayers with little or no federal income tax liability. Bills: H.R. 192, H.R. 713, H.R. 1332, H.R. 1333, H.R. 2334, H.R. 2956, H.R. 4722, S. 53, S. 18, S. 1869. Order No. R44420.

THE CHILD SUPPORT ENFORCEMENT PROGRAM: A LEGISLATIVE HISTORY, by Carmen Solomon-Fears, Specialist in Social Policy. 39 pages. March 21, 2016. The Child Support Enforcement (CSE) program was enacted in 1975 as a federal-state program (Title IV-D of the Social Security Act, P.L. 93-647). It is intended to help strengthen families by securing financial support for children from their noncustodial parent on a consistent and continuing basis and by helping some of these families to remain self-sufficient and off public assistance. Child support payments enable parents who do not live with their children to fulfill their financial responsibility to them by contributing to the payment of childrearing costs. Order No. R44423.

CHILD SUPPORT: AN OVERVIEW OF CENSUS BUREAU DATA ON RECIPIENTS, by Carmen Solomon-Fears, Specialist in Social Policy. 11 pages. Updated March 1, 2016. The U.S. Census Bureau periodically collects national survey information on child support. By interviewing a random sample of single-parent families, the Census Bureau is able to generate an array of data that is useful in assessing the performance of noncustodial parents in paying their child support.1 Although the Census Bureau

has been collecting child support information in a special Child Support Supplement to the April Current Population Survey (CPS) biennially since 1978, the supplement survey has changed significantly over the years. According to the Census Bureau, the most recent data, from 2013, 2 are comparable only back to 1993. During the early years of the survey, information was collected only from custodial mothers. Beginning with the 1991 data, information was also collected from custodial fathers. This report presents unsegmented data with respect to custodial mothers and fathers (i.e., custodial parents' data). The survey population includes all persons who have their own children under the age of 21 living with them, while the other parent lives outside the household. Order No. RS22499.

IMPROVING CHILD NUTRITION INTEGRITY AND ACCESS ACT OF 2016: IN BRIEF, by Randy Alison Aussenberg, Specialist in Nutrition Assistance Policy. 11 pages. Updated March 15, 2016. This report offers some basic background on the last reauthorization, its expiration, and some of the policies in the Senate committee's legislation. Please see the Senate committee's resources for further details on the committee print and the legislative text. Bills: H.R. 1728, H.R. 2715, S. 1539, S. 1966. Order No. R44373.

CIVIL RIGHTS AND LIBERTIES

NONPROFIT CHALLENGES TO THE CONTRACEPTIVE COVERAGE REQUIREMENT: THE MEANING OF SUBSTANTIAL BURDENS ON RELIGIOUS EXERCISE UNDER THE RELIGIOUS FREEDOM RESTORATION ACT, by Cynthia Brown, Legislative Attorney. 21 pages. March 21, 2016. This report examines the current parameters on governmental restrictions on religious exercise. It discusses the history of federal protection offered under the Free Exercise Clause of the First Amendment and RFRA, and notes parallel protections available at the state level. It analyzes the current interpretations of RFRA as applied to the contraceptive coverage requirement of the ACA, including discussion of Hobby Lobby and a review of the lower courts' interpretations of the nonprofit challenges. Finally, the report highlights a range of issue areas of interest to Congress that may be affected by the Court's interpretation of RFRA. Order No. R44422.

IRAQ: POLITICS AND GOVERNANCE, by Kenneth Katzman, Specialist in Middle Eastern Affairs; Carla E. Humud, Analyst in Middle Eastern and African Affairs. 44 pages. Updated March 9, 2016. Iraq's sectarian and ethnic divisions-muted toward the end of the 2003-2011 U.S. military intervention in Iraq-have reemerged to fuel a major challenge to Iraq's stability and to U.S. policy in Iraq and the broader Middle East region. The resentment of Iraq's Sunni Arabs toward the Shiite-dominated central government facilitated the capture in 2014 of nearly one-third of Iraqi territory by the Sunni Islamist extremist group called the Islamic State (also known as the Islamic State of Iraq and the Levant, or ISIL). Iraq's Kurds have been separately embroiled in political and territorial disputes with Baghdad, although those differences have been subordinated to the common struggle against the Islamic State. U.S. officials assert that defeating the Islamic State will require the Iraqi government to gain the loyalty of more of Iraq's Sunnis and to resolve differences with the Kurdistan Regional Government (KRG). Prospects for greater inter-communal unity appeared to increase in 2014 with the replacement of former Prime Minister Nuri al-Maliki with another Prime Minister, Haydar al-Abbadi. Although both men are from the Shiite Islamist Da'wa Party, Abbadi appears more willing than was Maliki to compromise with Sunni interests and with those of the KRG. In November 2014, Baghdad and the KRG reached a temporary agreement on the KRG's exportation of oil separately from Baghdad, but that agreement

largely collapsed in mid-2015. Order No. RS21968.

CIVIL SERVICE

THE FEDERAL EMPLOYEES' COMPENSATION ACT (FECA): WORKERS' COMPENSATION FOR FEDERAL EMPLOYEES, by Scott Szymendera, Analyst in Disability Policy. 25 pages. Updated March 18, 2016. The Federal Employees' Compensation Act (FECA) is the workers' compensation program for federal employees. Like all workers' compensation programs, FECA pays disability, survivors, and medical benefits, without fault, to employees who are injured or become ill in the course of their federal employment and the survivors of employees killed on the job. The FECA program is administered by the Department of Labor (DOL) and the costs of benefits are paid by each employee's host agency. Employees of the U.S. Postal Service (USPS) currently comprise the largest group of FECA beneficiaries and are responsible for the largest share of FECA benefits. Bills: H.R. 2309, H.R. 2465, H.R. 1196, H.R. 15316, H.R. 3141, H.R. 3191, H.R. 12383, H.R. 10721, H.R. 13871. Order No. R42107.

COMMEMORATIONS

COMMEMORATIVE DAYS, WEEKS, AND MONTHS: BACKGROUND AND CURRENT PRACTICE, by Jacob R. Straus, Analyst on the Congress. 17 pages. March 25, 2016. This report provides information on commemorative legislation that recognizes a specific time period, and then it discusses options for Congress. First, the report summarizes the different types of commemorative time periods-federal holidays; patriotic and national observances; and commemorative days, weeks, and months. Second, it discusses the current rules in the House and Senate that govern this type of legislation. Finally, the report discusses options for Congress, including introducing legislation in the House and

Senate, and asking the president to issue a proclamation. Order No. R44431.

COMMUNICATIONS

THE CORPORATION FOR PUBLIC BROADCASTING: FEDERAL FUNDING AND ISSUES, by Glenn J. McLoughlin, Section Research Manager; Rita Tehan, Information Research Specialist. 12 pages. Updated March 8, 2016. The Corporation for Public Broadcasting (CPB) receives virtually all of its funding through federal appropriations; overall, about 15% of public television and 10% of radio broadcasting funding comes from the federal appropriations that CPB distributes. CPB's appropriation is allocated through a distribution formula established in its authorizing legislation and has historically received two-year advanced appropriations. Congressional policy makers are increasingly interested in the federal role in supporting CPB due to concerns over the federal debt, the role of the federal government funding for public radio and television, and whether public broadcasting provides a balanced and nuanced approach to covering news of national interest. It is also important to note that many congressional policy makers defend the federal role of funding public broadcasting. They contend that it provides news and information to large segments of the population that seek to understand complex policy issues in depth, and in particular for children's television broadcasting, has a significant and positive impact on early learning and education for children. Order No. RS22168.

CONGRESS

GRANTS WORK IN A CONGRESSIONAL OFFICE, by Julie Jennings, Senior Research Librarian. 24 pages. Updated March 24, 2016. This report does not constitute a blueprint for every office involved in grants and projects activity, nor does it present in-depth information about all aspects of staff activity in this area. The discussion describes some basics about the grants process and some of the approaches and techniques used by congressional offices in dealing with this type of constituent service. Order No. RL34035.

MONUMENTS AND MEMORIALS AUTHORIZED AND COMPLETED UNDER THE COMMEMORATIVE WORKS ACT IN THE DISTRICT OF COLUMBIA, by Jacob R. Straus, Analyst on the Congress. 30 pages. Updated March 25, 2016. This report contains a catalog of the 19 authorized works that have been completed and dedicated since 1986. For each memorial, the report provides a rationale for each authorized work, as expressed by a Member of Congress, as well as the statutory authority for its creation; and identifies the group or groups which sponsored the commemoration, the memorial's location, and the dedication date. A picture of each work is also included. The Appendix includes a map showing each completed memorial's location. Bills: H.R. 2879, S. 2370, S. 1543. Order No. R43743.

MONUMENTS AND MEMORIALS AUTHORIZED UNDER THE COMMEMORATIVE WORKS ACT IN THE DISTRICT OF COLUMBIA: CURRENT DEVELOPMENT OF IN-PROGRESS AND LAPSED WORKS, by Jacob R. Straus, Analyst on the Congress. 27 pages. Updated March 25, 2016. This report provides a status update on eight in-progress memorials and five memorials with lapsed authorizations. For each monument or memorial, the report provides a rationale for the work as expressed in the Congressional Record or a House or Senate committee report; its statutory authority; the group or groups sponsoring the commemoration; and the memorial's location (or proposed location), if known. A picture or rendering of each work is also included, when available. Order No. R43744.

CONGRESSIONAL LIAISON OFFICES OF SELECTED FEDERAL AGENCIES, by

Audrey Celeste Crane-Hirsch, Reference .Librarian. 41 pages. Updated March 16, 2016. This list of about 200 congressional liaison offices is intended to help congressional offices in placing telephone calls and addressing correspondence to government agencies. In each case, the information was supplied by the agency itself and is current as of the date of publication. Entries are arranged alphabetically in four sections: legislative branch; judicial branch; executive branch; and agencies, boards, and commissions. Specific telephone numbers for correspondence, publications, and fax transmissions have been provided for each applicable agency. When using fax, it is important to include the entire mailing address on a cover sheet, as many of the listed fax machines are not directly located in the liaison offices. A number of agency listings include an email address. When emailing agencies please remember to include your name, affiliation, phone number, and return address, to ensure a speedy response. Users should be aware that email is not a confidential means of transmission. This report was produced for congressional offices only. It will be updated frequently. Order No. 98-446

CUBA: ISSUES FOR THE 114TH CONGRESS, by Mark P. Sullivan, Specialist in Latin American Affairs. 78 pages. Updated March 15, 2016. Cuba remains a one-party communist state with a poor record on human rights. The country's political succession in 2006 from the long-ruling Fidel Castro to his brother Raúl was characterized by a remarkable degree of stability. In 2013, Raúl began his second and final five-year term, which is scheduled to end in February 2018, when he would be 86 years old. Castro has implemented a number of market-oriented economic policy changes over the past several years. A 2011 party congress laid out numerous economic goals that, if implemented, could significantly alter Cuba's state-dominated economic model; another party congress is expected in April 2016 that would likely focus on progress in implementing the 2011 guidelines and future economic measures. Few observers, however, expect the government to ease its tight control over the political system. While the government has released most long-term political prisoners, short-term detentions and harassment have increased significantly over the past several years, reflecting a change of tactics in repressing dissent. Bills: H.R. 274, H.R. 403, H.R. 735, H.R. 634, H.R. 664, H.R. 3238, H.R. 3055, H.R. 3687, H.R. 2577, H.R. 2578, H.R. 2772, H.R. 2995, H.R. 3128, H.R. 2466, H.R. 2937, H.R. 2029, H.R. 654, H.R. 2772, H.R. 570, H.R. 738, H.R. 1782, H.R. 3818, H.R. 1627, H.R. 274, H.R. 403, H.R. 635, H.R. 735, S. 757, S. 1705, S. 1999, S. 1725, S. 1388, S. 1489, S. 1356, S. 299, S. 491, S. 1543, S. 1389, S. 1910. Order No. R43926.

FIRST-TERM MEMBERS OF THE HOUSE OF REPRESENTATIVES AND SENATE, 64TH -113TH CONGRESS, by Jennifer E. Manning, Information Research Specialist; R. Eric Peterson, Specialist in American National Government; Erin Hemlin, Research Associate. 19 pages. Updated March 7, 2016. This report provides summary data on the number of Senators and Members of the House of Representatives who first entered Congress between the 64th Congress (1915-1917) and the 113th Congress (2013-2014). First-term membership is divided into two broad categories in each chamber: Members chosen prior to the convening of a Congress, and those chosen after a Congress convenes. The resulting data, combining pre-convening and post-convening first-term Members, provide a count of all Members who served a first term in the House or Senate. Order No. R41283

HOUSE COMMITTEE CHAIRS: CONSIDERATIONS, DECISIONS, AND ACTIONS AS ONE CONGRESS ENDS AND A NEW CONGRESS BEGINS, by Judy Schneider, Specialist on the Congress; Michael L. Koempel, Senior Specialist in American National Government. 29 pages. Updated March 3, 2016.

This report covers the period from the House's early organization meetings through the spring district work period, which normally occurs in March or April. The report will be updated after the 114th Congress convenes if House rules or practices affecting chair decisions and actions discussed here change substantively. Order No. RL34679.

LEGISLATIVE BRANCH APPROPRIATIONS: FREQUENTLY ASKED QUESTIONS, by Ida A. Brudnick, Specialist on the Congress. 8 pages. Updated March 9, 2016. This report responds to frequently asked questions about legislative branch appropriations. Frequently asked questions include the development, presentation, and consideration of the legislative branch budget requests; the legislative branch budget in historical perspective; recent actions, including the effect of sequestration; and items that are funded in this bill. For additional information, including information on the most recent legislative branch appropriations act, see CRS Report R43151, Legislative Branch: FY2014 Appropriations, by Ida A. Brudnick. Order No. R43397.

TRANSPORTATION SPENDING UNDER AN EARMARK BAN, by Robert S. Kirk and William J. Mallett, Specialists in Transportation Policy; David Randall Peterman, Analyst in Transportation Policy. 14 pages. March 17, 2016. Proposals in both the House and the Senate to ban earmarks may lead to changes in the way transportation funding decisions are made. This report explains what earmarks are and discusses their use in surface transportation finance. It then considers how federal highway, transit, and aviation funding might be distributed if such a ban goes into effect, and how members of Congress might influence the distribution. Order No. R41554.

CRIMINAL JUSTICE

PUBLIC TRUST AND LAW ENFORCEMENT-A BRIEF DISCUSSION FOR POLICY MAKERS, by Nathan James, Coordinator Analyst in Crime Policy. 27 pages. Updated March 22, 2016. This report provides a brief overview of police-community relations and how policymakers might be able to play a role in repairing what appears to be fraying trust between police and citizens. The report focuses solely on the relationship between the police and the communities they serve. It does not include a discussion of the lack of trust in or perceived discrimination by other parts of the criminal justice system (i.e., the grand jury system, prosecutions, or corrections). While there may be many factors that influence how different groups of people feel they are treated by the criminal justice system, a discussion of those factors is beyond the scope of this report. The report starts with an overview of data on public opinion of law enforcement. It then provides a brief discussion of federalism and why Congress does not have the authority to directly change state and local law enforcement practices. Next, the report reviews federal efforts to collect data on law enforcement's use of force and federal authority to investigate instances of police misconduct. This is followed by a review of what role DOJ might be able to play in facilitating improvements in police-community relations or making changes in state and local law enforcement policies. The report concludes with policy options for Congress to consider should policymakers decide to try to influence state and local law enforcement policy. Order No. R43904.

FOREIGN CORRUPT PRACTICES ACT (FCPA): CONGRESSIONAL INTEREST AND EXECUTIVE ENFORCEMENT, by Michael V. Seitzinger, Legislative Attorney. 11 pages. Updated March 15, 2016 During the mid-1970s investigations and administrative and legal actions against numerous domestic corporations revealed that the practice of making questionable or illegal payments by United States corporations to foreign government officials existed to some extent within the American business community.1 The legal and regulatory mechanisms for dealing with these payments had involved actions by the Securities and Exchange Commission (SEC) against public corporations for concealing from required public disclosure substantial payments made by the firm, including to foreign government officials. There was also the potential for an antitrust action for restraints of trade or fraud prosecutions by the Department of Justice (DOJ). Government officials and administrators contended that more direct prohibitions on foreign bribery and more detailed requirements concerning corporate recordkeeping and accountability were needed to deal effectively with the problem. The revelations of slush funds and secret payments by American corporations were stated to have affected adversely American foreign policy, damaged abroad the image of American democracy, and impaired public confidence in the financial integrity of American corporations. Bills: H.R. 616, H.R. 5366, H.R. 5837, H.R. 2152, H.R. 3531, H.R. 3588, H.R. 4178. Order No. R41466

DEFENSE ECONOMICS

ENERGY AND WATER DEVELOPMENT APPROPRIATIONS FOR DEFENSE NUCLEAR NONPROLIFERATION: IN BRIEF, by Mary Beth D. Nikitin, Specialist in Nonproliferation. 7 pages. March 8, 2016. The Defense Nuclear Nonproliferation (DNN) programs were reorganized for the FY2016 request. There are now two main mission areas under the DNN appropriation: the Defense Nuclear Nonproliferation Program and the Nuclear Counterterrorism and Incident Response Program (NCTIR). NCTIR was previously funded under Weapons Activities. According to the FY2016 budget justification, "These transfers align all NNSA funding to prevent, counter, and respond to nuclear proliferation and terrorism in one appropriation." Order No. R44413.

MULTIYEAR PROCUREMENT (MYP) AND BLOCK BUY CONTRACTING IN DEFENSE ACQUISITION: BACKGROUND AND ISSUES FOR CONGRESS, by Ronald O'Rourke, Specialist in Naval Affairs; Moshe Schwartz, Specialist in Defense Acquisition. 19 pages. Updated March 23, 2016. This report provides background information and issues for Congress on multiyear procurement (MYP) and block buy contracting (BBC), which are special contracting mechanisms that Congress permits the Department of Defense (DOD) to use for a limited number of defense acquisition programs. Compared to the standard or default approach of annual contracting, MYP and BBC have the potential for reducing weapon procurement costs by several percent. Potential issues for Congress concerning MYP and BBC include whether to use MYP and BBC in the future more frequently, less frequently, or about as frequently as they are currently used; and whether to create a permanent statute to govern the use of BBC, analogous to the permanent statute (10 U.S.C. 2306b) that governs the use of MYP. Congress's decisions on these issues could affect defense acquisition practices, defense funding requirements, and the defense industrial base. Bills: S. 815, S. 1587, H.R. 4986, H.R. 4739, H.R. 1119, H.R. 1735, S. 1376, S. 3254, H.R. 1960, H.R. 2685, S. 1558, H.R. 2029. Order No. R41909.

DEFENSE POLICY

COAST GUARD POLAR ICEBREAKER MODERNIZATION: BACKGROUND AND ISSUES FOR CONGRESS, by Ronald O'Rourke, Specialist in Naval Affairs. 45 pages. Updated March 21, 2016. This report provides background information and issues for Congress on the sustainment and modernization of the Coast Guard's polar icebreaker fleet. Coast Guard polar icebreakers perform a variety of missions supporting U.S. interests in polar regions. The operational U.S. polar icebreaking fleet currently consists of one heavy polar icebreaker, Polar Star, and one medium polar icebreaker, Healy. The issue for Congress is whether to approve, reject, or modify the Administration's plans for sustaining and modernizing the polar icebreaking fleet. Congress's decisions on this issue could affect Coast Guard funding requirements, the Coast Guard's ability to perform its polar missions, and the U.S. shipbuilding industrial base. This report does not cover the icebreakers that the Coast Guard operates on the Great Lakes. A separate CRS report covers procurement of general-purpose cutters for the Coast Guard. Another CRS report provides an overview of various issues relating to the Arctic. Bills: H.R. 2838, H.R. 3128, S. 1619, H.R. 1987, S. 1611, S. 1386, H.R. 1735, H.R. 4567. Order No. RL34391.

MULTIYEAR PROCUREMENT (MYP) AND BLOCK BUY CONTRACTING IN DEFENSE ACQUISITION: BACKGROUND AND ISSUES FOR CONGRESS, by Ronald O'Rourke, Specialist in Naval Affairs; Moshe Schwartz, Specialist in Defense Acquisition. 19 pages. Updated March 23, 2016. This report provides background information and issues for Congress on multiyear procurement (MYP) and block buy contracting (BBC), which are special contracting mechanisms that Congress permits the Department of Defense (DOD) to use for a limited number of defense acquisition programs. Compared to the standard or default approach of annual contracting, MYP and BBC have the potential for reducing weapon procurement costs by several percent. Potential issues for Congress concerning MYP and BBC include whether to use MYP and BBC in the future more frequently, less frequently, or about as frequently as they are currently used; and whether to create a permanent statute to govern the use of BBC, analogous to the permanent statute (10 U.S.C. 2306b) that governs the use of MYP. Congress's decisions on these issues could affect defense acquisition practices, defense funding requirements, and the defense industrial base. Bills: S. 815, S. 1587, H.R. 4986, H.R. 4739, H.R. 1119, H.R. 1735, S.

1376, S. 3254, H.R. 1960, H.R. 2685, S. 1558, H.R. 2029. Order No. R41909.

NAVY FORD (CVN-78) CLASS AIRCRAFT CARRIER PROGRAM: BACKGROUND AND ISSUES FOR CONGRESS, by Ronald O'Rourke, Specialist in Naval Affairs. 74 pages. Updated March 21, 2016. This report provides background information and potential oversight issues for Congress on the Gerald R. Ford (CVN-78) class aircraft carrier program. The Navy's proposed FY2016 budget requests a total of $2,633.1 million in procurement and advance procurement (AP) funding for CVN-78, CVN-79, and CVN-80, the first three ships in the program. Congress's decisions on the CVN-78 program could substantially affect Navy capabilities and funding requirements and the shipbuilding industrial base. Bills: H.R. 1815, H.R. 5122, H.R. 2647, H.R. 1540, H.R. 4310, H.R. 3304, H.R. 1735, S. 1356. Order No. RS20643.

NAVY IRREGULAR WARFARE AND COUNTERTERRORISM OPERATIONS: BACKGROUND AND ISSUES FOR CONGRESS, by Ronald O'Rourke, Specialist in Naval Affairs. 41 pages. Updated March 25, 2016. This report provides background information and potential issues for Congress on the Navy's irregular warfare (IW) and counterterrorism (CT) operations. The Navy's IW and CT activities pose a number of potential oversight issues for Congress, including how much emphasis to place on IW and CT activities in future Navy budgets. Congress's decisions regarding Navy IW and CT operations can affect Navy operations and funding requirements, and the implementation of the nation's overall IW and CT strategies. Order No. RS22373.

NAVY DDG-51 AND DDG-1000 DESTROYER PROGRAMS: BACKGROUND AND ISSUES FOR CONGRESS, by Ronald O'Rourke, Specialist in Naval Affairs. 46 pages. Updated March 10, 2015. This report presents background information and potential oversight issues for Congress on the Navy's Arleigh Burke (DDG-51) and Zumwalt (DDG-1000) class destroyer programs. The Navy's proposed FY2016 budget requests funding for the procurement of two DDG-51s, including the first of a new DDG-51 design variant called the Flight III design, which is to carry a new and more capable radar called the Air and Missile Defense Radar (AMDR). Decisions that Congress makes concerning destroyer procurement could substantially affect Navy capabilities and funding requirements, and the U.S. shipbuilding industrial base. Bills: H.R. 1735, H.R. 2685, H.R. 2029, H.R. 1286, H.R. 1815, S. 1376, S. 1558. Order No. RL32109.

NAVY FORCE STRUCTURE AND SHIPBUILDING PLANS: BACKGROUND AND ISSUES FOR CONGRESS, by Ronald O'Rourke, Specialist in Naval Affairs. 52 pages. Updated March 17, 2016. This report presents background information and issues for Congress concerning the Navy's ship force-structure goals and shipbuilding plans. The planned size of the Navy, the rate of Navy ship procurement, and the prospective affordability of the Navy's shipbuilding plans have been matters of concern for the congressional defense committees for the past several years. Decisions that Congress makes on Navy shipbuilding programs can substantially affect Navy capabilities and funding requirements, and the U.S. shipbuilding industrial base. Bills: H.R. 1735, H.R. 2685, H.R. 2029, H.R. 4435, H.R. 4546, H.R. 6523, H.R. 1540, H.R. 1735, S. 1376, S. 1558. Order No. RL32665

NAVY LASERS, RAILGUN, AND HYPERVELOCITY PROJECTILE: BACKGROUND AND ISSUES FOR CONGRESS, by Ronald O'Rourke, Specialist in Naval Affairs. 33 pages. Updated March 18, 2016. This report provides background information and issues for Congress on three potential new weapons that could improve the ability of Navy surface ships to defend themselves against enemy missiles-solid state lasers (SSLs), the electromagnetic railgun (EMRG), and the hypervelocity projectile (HVP). Bills: H.R. 1540. Order No. R44175

NAVY LX(R) AMPHIBIOUS SHIP PROGRAM: BACKGROUND AND ISSUES FOR CONGRESS, by Ronald O'Rourke, Specialist in Naval Affairs. 13 pages. Updated March 16, 2016. This report provides background information and issues for Congress on the LX(R) amphibious ship program, a Navy program to build a new class of 11 amphibious ships. The Navy wants to procure the first LX(R) in FY2020. The LX(R) program raises a number of oversight issues for Congress. Decisions Congress makes on the LX(R) program will affect Navy capabilities and funding requirements, and the U.S. shipbuilding industrial base. Bills: H.R. 1735, S. 1376, H.R. 2685, S. 1558, H.R. 2029, Order No. R43543.

NAVY VIRGINIA (SSN-774) CLASS ATTACK SUBMARINE PROCUREMENT: BACKGROUND AND ISSUES FOR CONGRESS, by Ronald O'Rourke, Specialist in Naval Affairs. 33 pages. Updated March 9, 2016. This report provides background information and issues for Congress on the Virginia-class nuclear-powered attack submarine (SSN) program. The Navy's proposed FY2017 budget requests $4,955.2 million in procurement and advance procurement (AP) funding for the program. Decisions that Congress makes on procurement of Virginia-class boats could substantially affect U.S. Navy capabilities and funding requirements, and the U.S. shipbuilding industrial base. The Navy's Ohio Replacement (SSBN[X]) ballistic missile submarine program is discussed in another CRS report. Bills: H.R. 1735, H.R. 2685, H.R. 2029, H.R. 3547, S. 1376, S. 1558. Order No. RL32418.

U.S. STRATEGIC NUCLEAR FORCES: BACKGROUND, DEVELOPMENTS, AND ISSUES, by Amy F. Woolf, Specialist in Nuclear Weapons Policy. 49 pages. Updated March 10,

2016. This report reviews the ongoing programs that will affect the expected size and shape of the U.S. strategic nuclear force structure. It begins with an overview of this force structure during the Cold War, and summarizes the reductions and changes that have occurred since 1991. It then offers details about each category of delivery vehicle-land-based intercontinental ballistic missiles (ICBMs), submarine launched ballistic missiles (SLBMs), and heavy bombers-focusing on their current deployments and ongoing and planned modernization programs. The report concludes with a discussion of issues related to decisions about the future size and shape of the U.S. strategic nuclear force. Order No. RL33640.

NATIONAL DEFENSE

NONSTRATEGIC NUCLEAR WEAPONS, by Amy F. Woolf, Specialist in Nuclear Weapons Policy. 41 pages. Updated March 23, 2016. This report provides basic information about U.S. and Russian nonstrategic nuclear weapons. It begins with a brief discussion of how these weapons have appeared in public debates in the past few decades, then summarizes the differences between strategic and nonstrategic nuclear weapons. It then provides some historical background, describing the numbers and types of nonstrategic nuclear weapons deployed by both nations during the Cold War and in the past decade; the policies that guided the deployment and prospective use of these weapons; and the measures that the two sides have taken to reduce and contain their forces. The report reviews the issues that have been raised with regard to U.S. and Russian nonstrategic nuclear weapons, and summarizes a number of policy options that might be explored by Congress, the United States, Russia, and other nations to address these issues. Bills: H.R. 4310, H.R. 5017, H.R. 1. Order No. RL32572.

NAVY JOHN LEWIS (TAO-205) CLASS OILER SHIPBUILDING PROGRAM: BACKGROUND AND ISSUES FOR CONGRESS, by Ronald O'Rourke, Specialist in Naval Affairs. 24 pages. Updated March 15, 2016. This report provides background information and issues for Congress on the John Lewis (TAO-205) class oiler shipbuilding program, a program to build a new class of 17 fleet oilers for the Navy. The TAO-205 program was previously known as the TAO(X) program. The first ship in the program was funded in FY2016 at a cost of $674.2 million. The Navy's proposed FY2017 budget requests $73.1 million in advance procurement (AP) funding for the second ship, which the Navy wants to procure in FY2018. Bills: H.R. 1735, S. 1376, H.R. 2685, S. 1558, H.R. 2029. Order No. R43546

NAVY LX(R) AMPHIBIOUS SHIP PROGRAM: BACKGROUND AND ISSUES FOR CONGRESS, by Ronald O'Rourke, Specialist in Naval Affairs. 13 pages. Updated March 16, 2016. This report provides background information and issues for Congress on the LX(R) amphibious ship program, a Navy program to build a new class of 11 amphibious ships. The Navy wants to procure the first LX(R) in FY2020. The LX(R) program raises a number of oversight issues for Congress. Decisions Congress makes on the LX(R) program will affect Navy capabilities and funding requirements, and the U.S. shipbuilding industrial base. Bills: H.R. 1735, S. 1376, H.R. 2685, S. 1558, H.R. 2029. Order No. R43543.

WEAPONS SYSTEMS

ENERGY AND WATER DEVELOPMENT APPROPRIATIONS FOR DEFENSE NUCLEAR NONPROLIFERATION: IN BRIEF, by Mary Beth D. Nikitin, Specialist in Nonproliferation. 7 pages. March 8, 2016. The Defense Nuclear Nonproliferation (DNN) programs were reorganized for the FY2016 request. There are now two main mission areas under the DNN appropriation: the Defense Nuclear Nonproliferation Program and the Nuclear Counterterrorism and Incident Response

Program (NCTIR). NCTIR was previously funded under Weapons Activities. According to the FY2016 budget justification, "These transfers align all NNSA funding to prevent, counter, and respond to nuclear proliferation and terrorism in one appropriation." Order No. R44413.

NAVY FORD (CVN-78) CLASS AIRCRAFT CARRIER PROGRAM: BACKGROUND AND ISSUES FOR CONGRESS, by Ronald O'Rourke, Specialist in Naval Affairs. 74 pages. Updated March 21, 2016. This report provides background information and potential oversight issues for Congress on the Gerald R. Ford (CVN-78) class aircraft carrier program. The Navy's proposed FY2016 budget requests a total of $2,633.1 million in procurement and advance procurement (AP) funding for CVN-78, CVN-79, and CVN-80, the first three ships in the program. Congress's decisions on the CVN-78 program could substantially affect Navy capabilities and funding requirements and the shipbuilding industrial base. Bills: H.R. 1815, H.R. 5122, H.R. 2647, H.R. 1540, H.R. 4310, H.R. 3304, H.R. 1735, S. 1356. Order No. RS20643.

NONSTRATEGIC NUCLEAR WEAPONS, by Amy F. Woolf, Specialist in Nuclear Weapons Policy. 41 pages. Updated March 23, 2016. This report provides basic information about U.S. and Russian nonstrategic nuclear weapons. It begins with a brief discussion of how these weapons have appeared in public debates in the past few decades, then summarizes the differences between strategic and nonstrategic nuclear weapons. It then provides some historical background, describing the numbers and types of nonstrategic nuclear weapons deployed by both nations during the Cold War and in the past decade; the policies that guided the deployment and prospective use of these weapons; and the measures that the two sides have taken to reduce and contain their forces. The report reviews the issues that have been raised with regard to U.S. and Russian nonstrategic nuclear weapons, and summarizes a number of policy options that

might be explored by Congress, the United States, Russia, and other nations to address these issues. Bills: H.R. 4310, H.R. 5017, H.R. 1. Order No. RL32572.

NAVY DDG-51 AND DDG-1000 DESTROYER PROGRAMS: BACKGROUND AND ISSUES FOR CONGRESS, by Ronald O'Rourke, Specialist in Naval Affairs. 46 pages. Updated March 10, 2015. This report presents background information and potential oversight issues for Congress on the Navy's Arleigh Burke (DDG-51) and Zumwalt (DDG-1000) class destroyer programs. The Navy's proposed FY2016 budget requests funding for the procurement of two DDG-51s, including the first of a new DDG-51 design variant called the Flight III design, which is to carry a new and more capable radar called the Air and Missile Defense Radar (AMDR). Decisions that Congress makes concerning destroyer procurement could substantially affect Navy capabilities and funding requirements, and the U.S. shipbuilding industrial base. Bills: H.R. 1735, H.R. 2685, H.R. 2029, H.R. 1286, H.R. 1815, S. 1376, S. 1558. Order No. RL32109.

NAVY LX(R) AMPHIBIOUS SHIP PROGRAM: BACKGROUND AND ISSUES FOR CONGRESS, by Ronald O'Rourke, Specialist in Naval Affairs. 13 pages. Updated March 16, 2016. This report provides background information and issues for Congress on the LX(R) amphibious ship program, a Navy program to build a new class of 11 amphibious ships. The Navy wants to procure the first LX(R) in FY2020. The LX(R) program raises a number of oversight issues for Congress. Decisions Congress makes on the LX(R) program will affect Navy capabilities and funding requirements, and the U.S. shipbuilding industrial base. Bills: H.R. 1735, S. 1376, H.R. 2685, S. 1558, H.R. 2029. Order No. R43543.

U.S. STRATEGIC NUCLEAR FORCES: BACKGROUND, DEVELOPMENTS, AND ISSUES, by Amy F. Woolf, Specialist in Nuclear Weapons Policy. 49 pages. Updated March 10,

2016. This report reviews the ongoing programs that will affect the expected size and shape of the U.S. strategic nuclear force structure. It begins with an overview of this force structure during the Cold War, and summarizes the reductions and changes that have occurred since 1991. It then offers details about each category of delivery vehicle-land-based intercontinental ballistic missiles (ICBMs), submarine launched ballistic missiles (SLBMs), and heavy bombers-focusing on their current deployments and ongoing and planned modernization programs. The report concludes with a discussion of issues related to decisions about the future size and shape of the U.S. strategic nuclear force. Order No. RL33640.

DISABLED PERSONS

SECTION 811 AND OTHER HUD HOUSING PROGRAMS FOR PERSONS WITH DISABILITIES, by Libby Perl, Specialist in Housing Policy. 36 pages. Updated March 7, 2016. This report describes how federal funds are used to develop housing designated for persons with disabilities. It also discusses recent funding for the Section 811 program and current issues surrounding housing for persons with disabilities, including mixed financing arrangements, worst case housing needs, and persons with disabilities who are homeless. Bills: H.R. 12433, H.R. 4, H.R. 5576, H.R. 1158, S. 3084. Order No. RL34728.

THE INDIVIDUALS WITH DISABILITIES EDUCATION ACT (IDEA), PART B: KEY STATUTORY AND REGULATORY PROVISIONS, by Kyrie E. Dragoo, Analyst in Education Policy. 33 pages. Updated March 11, 2016. The focus of this report will be on how these purposes are to be achieved under Part B of the IDEA, hereinafter referred to as IDEA. The first purpose is addressed primarily in the section of this report titled "Services for Children with Disabilities." The second is addressed in the section on "Procedural Safeguards," and the third is addressed in the section on "Funding,

Expenditure Requirements, and Compliance." Order No. R41833.

DISTRICT OF COLUMBIA

MONUMENTS AND MEMORIALS AUTHORIZED AND COMPLETED UNDER THE COMMEMORATIVE WORKS ACT IN THE DISTRICT OF COLUMBIA, by Jacob R. Straus, Analyst on the Congress. 30 pages. Updated March 25, 2016. This report contains a catalog of the 19 authorized works that have been completed and dedicated since 1986. For each memorial, the report provides a rationale for each authorized work, as expressed by a Member of Congress, as well as the statutory authority for its creation; and identifies the group or groups which sponsored the commemoration, the memorial's location, and the dedication date. A picture of each work is also included. The Appendix includes a map showing each completed memorial's location. Bills: H.R. 2879, S. 2370, S. 1543. Order No. R43743.

MONUMENTS AND MEMORIALS AUTHORIZED UNDER THE COMMEMORATIVE WORKS ACT IN THE DISTRICT OF COLUMBIA: CURRENT DEVELOPMENT OF IN-PROGRESS AND LAPSED WORKS, by Jacob R. Straus, Analyst on the Congress. 27 pages. Updated March 25, 2016. This report provides a status update on eight in-progress memorials and five memorials with lapsed authorizations. For each monument or memorial, the report provides a rationale for the work as expressed in the Congressional Record or a House or Senate committee report; its statutory authority; the group or groups sponsoring the commemoration; and the memorial's location (or proposed location), if known. A picture or rendering of each work is also included, when available. Order No. R43744.

ECONOMIC POLICY

REAL ESTATE INVESTMENT TRUSTS (REITS) AND THE FOREIGN INVESTMENT IN REAL PROPERTY TAX ACT (FIRPTA): OVERVIEW AND RECENT TAX REVISIONS, by Jane G. Gravelle, Senior Specialist in Economic Policy. 15 pages. March 22, 2016. This report describes REITs and FIRPTA, provides historical developments, presents an overview of REIT size and activity, explains the provisions in the Consolidated Appropriations Act, and discusses possible policy issues in the future. Bills: H.R. 1, H.R. 2029, Order No. R44421.

Education

CAMPUS-BASED STUDENT FINANCIAL AID PROGRAMS UNDER THE HIGHER EDUCATION ACT, by Alexandra Hegji, Analyst in Social Policy; David P. Smole, Specialist in Education Policy. 27 pages. Updated February 29, 2016. This report describes the FSEOG, FWS, and Federal Perkins Loan programs, as amended by the HEOA. It also presents historical information on appropriations provided for the programs and the federal student aid that has been made available to students through the programs. Order No. RL31618.

ESEA TITLE I-A FORMULAS: IN BRIEF, by Rebecca R. Skinner, Specialist in Education Policy. 10 pages. Updated March 7, 2016. This report provides a summary of key changes to the Title I-A formulas proposed in the Student Success Act (H.R. 5), as passed by the House, and the Every Child Achieves Act of 2015 (S. 1177), as passed by the Senate. Both bills would provide for a comprehensive reauthorization of the ESEA and would make changes to the distribution of funds under Title I-A. H.R. 5 would change the distribution of funds to LEAs and schools after ED has calculated grant amounts using the aforementioned formulas. S. 1177 would alter the distribution of funds from LEAs to schools and would add an additional formula to the four existing Title I-A formulas. Bills: H.R. 5, S. 1177. Order No. R44164.

SCHOOL MEALS PROGRAMS AND OTHER USDA CHILD NUTRITION PROGRAMS: A PRIMER, by Randy Alison Aussenberg, Specialist in Nutrition Assistance Policy. 43 pages. Updated March 15, 2016. This report presents an overview of the benefits and services these programs and related activities provide as well as participation and funding information. The report emphasizes details for the school meals programs and provides an orientation to the operations of the other programs. Bills: H.R. 1728, H.R. 2715, S. 1539, S. 613, S. 1966. Order No. R43783.

THE INDIVIDUALS WITH DISABILITIES EDUCATION ACT (IDEA), PART B: KEY STATUTORY AND REGULATORY PROVISIONS, by Kyrie E. Dragoo, Analyst in Education Policy. 33 pages. Updated March 11, 2016. The focus of this report will be on how these purposes are to be achieved under Part B of the IDEA, hereinafter referred to as IDEA. The first purpose is addressed primarily in the section of this report titled "Services for Children with Disabilities." The second is addressed in the section on "Procedural Safeguards," and the third is addressed in the section on "Funding, Expenditure Requirements, and Compliance." Order No. R41833.

THE INDIVIDUALS WITH DISABILITIES EDUCATION ACT (IDEA), PART B: KEY STATUTORY AND REGULATORY PROVISIONS, by Kyrie E. Dragoo, Analyst in Education Policy. 33 pages. Updated March 11, 2016. The focus of this report will be on how these purposes are to be achieved under Part B of the IDEA, hereinafter referred to as IDEA. The first purpose is addressed primarily in the section of this report titled "Services for Children with Disabilities." The second is addressed in the section on "Procedural Safeguards," and the third is addressed in the section on "Funding,

Expenditure Requirements, and Compliance." Order No. R41833.

ELDERLY PEOPLE

MEDICARE: PART B PREMIUMS, by Patricia A. Davis, Specialist in Health Care Financing. 48 pages. Updated March 25, 2016. Medicare is a federal insurance program that pays for covered health care services of most individuals aged 65 and older and certain disabled persons. In 2016, the program is expected to cover about 57 million persons (48 million aged and 9 million disabled) at a total cost of $688 billion. Most individuals (or their spouses) aged 65 and older who have worked in covered employment and paid Medicare payroll taxes for 40 quarters receive premium-free Medicare Part A (Hospital Insurance). Those entitled to Medicare Part A (regardless of whether they are eligible for premium-free Part A) have the option of enrolling in Part B, which covers such things as physician and outpatient services and medical equipment. Bills: H.R. 1418, H.R. 1314, H.R. 2, H.R. 3696, H.R. 4090, H.R. 2476, H.R. 1654, H.R. 2235, S. 1453, S. 1961. Order No. R40082.

SECTION 202 AND OTHER HUD RENTAL HOUSING PROGRAMS FOR LOW-INCOME ELDERLY RESIDENTS, by Libby Perl, Specialist in Housing Policy. 30 pages. Updated March 7, 2016. This report provides a summary of the HUD programs that provide multi-family rental housing for low-income elderly households and their related supportive services programs. It also discusses funding and current issues in the area of assisted housing for low-income elderly persons. However, the report does not include a comprehensive look at all housing programs that serve elderly households. Major sources of assistance that are not discussed include HUD's Section 8 voucher program,7 HUD's mortgage insurance and reverse mortgage programs,8 and the Department of Agriculture's rural housing programs that provide assistance to elderly households. Bills: H.R. 8, H.R. 5, H.R. 3, H.R. 31, S. 566. Order No. RL33508.

EMERGENCY MANAGEMENT

FIVE YEARS OF THE BUDGET CONTROL ACT'S DISASTER RELIEF ADJUSTMENT, by William L. Painter, Analyst in Emergency Management and Homeland Security Policy. 19 pages. March 15, 2016. This report examines how the adjustment has functioned over the first five years, and what the future of disaster relief (as defined by the BCA) may look like for the next five years and beyond. Under current law, the allowable adjustment is expected to decline from a high of almost $18.5 billion in FY2015 to between $7.5 billion and $9.5 billion by the time the BCA discretionary spending limits expire after FY2021. Bills: H.R. 2467. Order No. R44415

ENERGY

ELECTRICITY MARKETS-RECENT ISSUES IN MARKET STRUCTURE AND ENERGY TRADING, by Richard J. Campbell, Specialist in Energy Policy. 37 pages. Updated March 21, 2016. The electricity industry is entering a time of change, and electricity markets are evolving with the industry. The expected retirement of many coal-fired power plants can affect RTO markets as generator portfolios change to include more natural gas-fired plants, and the prices that this new generation is expected to command. With load growth stagnant in many regions, the pull towards a greater use of hedging and more liquid markets may increase as the need to decrease costs and stabilize revenues increases. Congress may choose to consider whether to change how RTO electricity markets are regulated and operated (i.e., through some standardization of these markets or elements in these markets), with an eye towards improving efficiency, and increasing regulatory clarity and transparency, lowering costs, and thus potentially reducing opportunities for fraud or market manipulation. Order No. R43093.

ENERGY AND WATER DEVELOPMENT APPROPRIATIONS FOR DEFENSE NUCLEAR NONPROLIFERATION: IN BRIEF, by Mary Beth D. Nikitin, Specialist in Nonproliferation. 7 pages. March 8, 2016. The Defense Nuclear Nonproliferation (DNN) programs were reorganized for the FY2016 request. There are now two main mission areas under the DNN appropriation: the Defense Nuclear Nonproliferation Program and the Nuclear Counterterrorism and Incident Response Program (NCTIR). NCTIR was previously funded under Weapons Activities. According to the FY2016 budget justification, "These transfers align all NNSA funding to prevent, counter, and respond to nuclear proliferation and terrorism in one appropriation." Order No. R44413

ENVIRONMENTAL PROTECTION

CLEAN WATER ACT SECTION 401: BACKGROUND AND ISSUES, by Claudia Copeland, Specialist in Resources and Environmental Policy. 10 pages. Updated March 7, 2016. Under the Clean Water Act (CWA), an applicant for a federal license or permit to conduct any activity that may result in a discharge to waters of the United States must provide the federal agency with a Section 401 certification. The certification, made by the state in which the discharge originates, declares that the discharge will comply with applicable provisions of the act, including water quality standards. A state's water quality standards specify the designated use of a stream or lake (e.g., for water supply or recreation), pollutant limits necessary to protect the designated use (in the form of numeric or narrative criteria), and policies to ensure that existing water uses will not be degraded by pollutant discharges. Bills: H.R. 8, H.R. 961, H.R. 2018, S. 2012, S. 2093. Order No. 97-488.

WATER POLLUTION

CLEAN WATER ACT SECTION 401: BACKGROUND AND ISSUES, by Claudia Copeland, Specialist in Resources and Environmental Policy. 10 pages. Updated March 7, 2016. Under the Clean Water Act (CWA), an applicant for a federal license or permit to conduct any activity that may result in a discharge to waters of the United States must provide the federal agency with a Section 401 certification. The certification, made by the state in which the discharge originates, declares that the discharge will comply with applicable provisions of the act, including water quality standards. A state's water quality standards specify the designated use of a stream or lake (e.g., for water supply or recreation), pollutant limits necessary to protect the designated use (in the form of numeric or narrative criteria), and policies to ensure that existing water uses will not be degraded by pollutant discharges. Bills: H.R. 8, H.R. 961, H.R. 2018, S. 2012, S. 2093. Order No. 97-488.

WATER INFRASTRUCTURE FINANCING: HISTORY OF EPA APPROPRIATIONS, by Claudia Copeland, Specialist in Resources and Environmental Policy. 37 pages. Updated February 29, 2016. The principal federal program to aid municipal wastewater treatment plant construction is authorized in the Clean Water Act (CWA). Established as a grant program in 1972, it now capitalizes state loan programs. Authorizations since 1972 have totaled $65 billion, while appropriations have totaled nearly $90 billion. It has represented 25%-30% of total funds appropriated to the Environmental Protection Agency (EPA) in recent years. In appropriations legislation, funding for EPA wastewater assistance is contained in the measure providing funds for the Department of the Interior, Environment, and Related Agencies, which includes EPA. Within the portion of that bill which funds EPA, wastewater treatment assistance is specified in an account now called

State and Tribal Assistance Grants (STAG). Three trends in the funding of this account are most prominent: inclusion of non-infrastructure environmental grants to states, beginning in FY1993; increasing number and amount of special purpose grants since FY1989; and the addition of grant assistance for drinking water treatment projects in FY1997. This report summarizes, in chronological order, congressional activity to fund items in this account since 1987. Bills: H.R. 4624, H.R. 3666, H.R. 2158, H.R. 2684, H.R. 2099, H.R. 3019, H.R. 4194, S. 2168, S. 1034, S. 1216. Order No. 96-647.

EXECUTIVE BRANCH DEPARTMENTS

CONGRESSIONAL LIAISON OFFICES OF SELECTED FEDERAL AGENCIES, by Audrey Celeste Crane-Hirsch, Reference Librarian. 41 pages. Updated March 16, 2016. This list of about 200 congressional liaison offices is intended to help congressional offices in placing telephone calls and addressing correspondence to government agencies. In each case, the information was supplied by the agency itself and is current as of the date of publication. Entries are arranged alphabetically in four sections: legislative branch; judicial branch; executive branch; and agencies, boards, and commissions. Specific telephone numbers for correspondence, publications, and fax transmissions have been provided for each applicable agency. When using fax, it is important to include the entire mailing address on a cover sheet, as many of the listed fax machines are not directly located in the liaison offices. A number of agency listings include an email address. When emailing agencies please remember to include your name, affiliation, phone number, and return address, to ensure a speedy response. Users should be aware that email is not a confidential means of transmission. This report was produced for congressional offices only. It will be updated frequently. Order No. 98-446

FAMILIES

TITLE X (PUBLIC HEALTH SERVICE ACT) FAMILY PLANNING PROGRAM, by Angela Napili, Information Research Specialist. 22 pages. Updated March 15, 2016. The federal government provides grants for voluntary family planning services through the Family Planning Program, Title X of the Public Health Service Act (42 U.S.C. §§300 to 300a-6). Enacted in 1970, it is the only domestic federal program devoted solely to family planning and related preventive health services. In 2014, Title X-funded clinics served 4.1 million clients. Title X is administered through the Office of Population Affairs (OPA) in the Department of Health and Human Services (HHS). Although the authorization of appropriations for Title X ended with FY1985, funding for the program has continued through appropriations bills for the Departments of Labor, Health and Human Services, and Education, and Related Agencies (Labor-HHS-Education). The FY2015 Consolidated and Further Continuing Appropriations Act (P.L. 113-235) provided $286 million for Title X, the same as the FY2014 level. The FY2015 act continued previous years' requirements that Title X funds not be spent on abortions, that all pregnancy counseling be nondirective, and that funds not be spent on promoting or opposing any legislative proposal or candidate for public office. Grantees continued to be required to certify that they encourage "family participation" when minors seek family planning services and to certify that they counsel minors on how to resist attempted coercion into sexual activity. The appropriations law also clarified that family planning providers are not exempt from state notification and reporting laws on child abuse, child molestation, sexual abuse, rape, or incest. Bills: H.R. 2764, H.R. 1105. Order No. RL33644.

FINANCE

ARGENTINA: BACKGROUND AND U.S. RELATIONS, by Mark P. Sullivan, Specialist in Latin American Affairs; Rebecca M. Nelson, Specialist in International Trade and Finance. 25 pages. Updated March 22, 2016. Argentina, a South American country with a population of almost 42 million, has had a vibrant democratic tradition since its military relinquished power in 1983. Current President Cristina Fernández de Kirchner, from a center-left faction of the Peronist party, the Front for Victory (FPV), was first elected in 2007 (succeeding her husband, Néstor Kirchner, who served one term) and is now in the final months of her second term. Argentina's constitution does not allow for more than two successive terms, so President Fernández is ineligible to run in the next presidential election, with a first round scheduled for October 25, 2015. Eleven candidates competed in an August 9, 2015, combined open primary for electoral alliances, and three top candidates emerged: Daniel Scioli, governor of Buenos Aires province under the banner of President Fernández's FPV; Mauricio Macri, mayor of Buenos Aires, heading the Let's Change coalition that includes center-right and center-left opposition parties; and Sergio Massa, a deputy in Argentina's Congress, who heads a centrist dissident Peronist faction known as United for a New Alternative. This report provides background on the political and economic situation in Argentina and U.S.-Argentine relations.

This report provides background on the political and economic situation in Argentina and U.S.-Argentine relations. An Appendix provides links to selected U.S. government reports on Argentina. Bills: H.R. 3049, S.1800. Order No. R43816.

CURRENT DEBATES OVER EXCHANGE RATES: OVERVIEW AND ISSUES FOR CONGRESS, by Rebecca M. Nelson, Specialist in International Trade and Finance. 30 pages. Updated March 22, 2016. This report provides information on current debates over exchange rates in the global economy. It offers an overview of how exchange rates work; analyzes specific disagreements and debates; and examines existing frameworks for potentially addressing currency disputes. It also lays out some policy options available to Congress, should Members want to take action on exchange rate issues. Bills: H.R. 820, H.R. 2378, H.R. 2942, S. 433, S. 1269, S. 1619. Order No. R43242.

FINANCING AIRPORT IMPROVEMENTS, by Rachel Y. Tang, Analyst in Transportation and Industry; Robert S. Kirk, Specialist in Transportation Policy. 30 pages. Updated March 24, 2016. There are five major sources of airport capital development funding: the federal Airport Improvement Program (AIP); local passenger facility charges (PFCs) imposed pursuant to federal law; tax-exempt bonds; state and local grants; and airport operating revenue from tenant lease and other revenue generating activities such as landing fees. Federal involvement is most consequential in AIP, PFCs, and tax-exempt financing. This report provides an overview of airport improvement financing, with emphasis on AIP and the related passenger facility charges. It also discusses some ongoing airport issues that are likely to be included in a future FAA reauthorization debate. Bills: H.R. 4721. Order No. R43327.

FHA-INSURED HOME LOANS: AN OVERVIEW, by Katie Jones, Analyst in Housing Policy. 20 pages. Updated March 16, 2016. This report provides background on FHA's history and market role and an overview of the basic eligibility and underwriting criteria for FHA-insured home loans. It also provides data on the number and dollar volume of mortgages that FHA insures, along with data on FHA's market share in recent years. It does not go into detail on the financial status of the FHA mortgage insurance fund; for information on FHA's financial position, see CRS Report R42875, FHA Single-Family Mortgage Insurance: Financial Status of the Mutual Mortgage Insurance Fund (MMI Fund), by Katie Jones. Recent FHA policy changes are discussed in CRS Report R43531, FHA Single- Family Mortgage Insurance: Recent Policy Changes and Proposed Legislation, by Katie Jones. Order No. RS20530.

INTERNATIONAL TRADE AND FINANCE: KEY POLICY ISSUES FOR THE 114TH CONGRESS, by Mary A. Irace, Coordinator Section Research Manager; Brock R. Williams, Coordinator Analyst in International Trade and Finance. 38 pages. Updated February 29, 2016. Congress is in a unique position to address these issues, particularly given its constitutional authority for legislating and overseeing international trade and financial policy. This report provides a brief overview of some of the trade and finance issues that may come before the second session of the 114th Congress. Appendix A provides a list of CRS products covering these issues in greater detail. Bills: H.R. 1191, H.R. 2297, H.R. 757, H.R. 3662, H.R. 644, S. 284, S. 433. Order No. R43841.

SMALL BUSINESS: ACCESS TO CAPITAL AND JOB CREATION, by Robert Jay Dilger, Senior Specialist in American National Government. 33 pages. Updated March 1, 2016. The U.S. Small Business Administration (SBA) administers several programs to support small businesses, including loan guaranty and venture capital programs to enhance small business access to capital; contracting programs to increase small business opportunities in federal contracting; direct loan programs for businesses, homeowners, and renters to assist their recovery from natural disasters; and small business management and technical assistance training programs to assist business formation and expansion. Congressional interest in these programs has increased in recent years, primarily because assisting small business is viewed as a means to enhance economic growth. Bills: H.R. 5851, H.R. 2499, H.R. 3584, H.R. 3007, H.R. 5835, H.R. 2451, H.R. 35854, S. 1828. Order No. R40985

STATE SMALL BUSINESS CREDIT INITIATIVE: IMPLEMENTATION AND FUNDING ISSUES, by Robert Jay Dilger, Senior Specialist in American National Government. 43 pages. Updated March 17, 2016. This report examines the SSBCI and its implementation, including Treasury's response to initial program audits conducted by the U.S. Government Accountability Office (GAO) and Treasury's Office of Inspector General (OIG). These initial audits suggest that SSBCI participants are generally complying with the statute's requirements but that some compliance problems exist. They also indicate that Treasury's oversight of the program could be improved and that performance measures are needed to assess the program's efficacy. Bills: H.R. 4556, H.R. 5297, H.R. 5302, H.R. 5297, H.R. 5486, S. 2285. Order No. R42581

TAX REFORM IN THE 114TH CONGRESS: AN OVERVIEW OF PROPOSALS, by Molly F. Sherlock, Coordinator of Division Research and Specialist. 24 pages. Updated March 18, 2016. On December 10, 2014, the Chairman of the House Committee on Ways and Means introduced a comprehensive tax reform proposal, the Tax Reform Act of 2014 (H.R. 1). The bill proposed substantial changes to both the individual and corporate income tax systems, reducing statutory tax rates for many taxpayers, while repealing dozens of credits, deductions, and other tax preferences. While no further action was taken on H.R. 1 in the 113th Congress, the proposal continues to inform the ongoing tax reform debate. Bills: H.R. 1, H.R. 25, H.R. 1040, H.R. 1824, H.R. 25, S. 155, S. 929. Order No. R43060

TRANSATLANTIC TRADE AND INVESTMENT PARTNERSHIP (TTIP) NEGOTIATIONS, by Shayerah Ilias Akhtar, Specialist in International Trade and Finance; Vivian C. Jones, Specialist in International Trade and Finance. 61 pages. Updated February 29, 2016. This report provides: (1) context for the T-

TIP negotiations; (2) analysis of possible trade and investment issues in the negotiations; and (3) discussion of issues for Congress. The U.S.-EU negotiations on T-TIP are not public. The information and analysis in this report on issues in the negotiations are based on publicly available information. Bills: H.R. 644. Order No. R43387

FOOD

COUNTRY-OF-ORIGIN LABELING FOR FOODS AND THE WTO TRADE DISPUTE ON MEAT LABELING, by Joel L. Greene, Analyst in Agricultural Policy. 62 pages. Updated March 8, 2016. Since the final rule to implement country-of-origin labeling (COOL) took effect in March 2009, most retail food stores have been required to inform consumers about the country of origin of fresh fruits and vegetables, fish, shellfish, peanuts, pecans, macadamia nuts, ginseng, and ground and muscle cuts of beef, pork, lamb, chicken, and goat. The rules are required by the 2002 farm bill (P.L. 107-171) as amended by the 2008 farm bill (P.L. 110-246). Other U.S. laws have required such labeling, but only for imported food products already pre-packaged for consumers. Canada and Mexico challenged U.S. COOL in the World Trade Organization (WTO), arguing that COOL has a trade-distorting impact by reducing the value and number of cattle and hogs shipped to the U.S. market, thus violating WTO trade commitments. In November 2011, the WTO dispute settlement (DS) panel found that COOL treats imported livestock less favorably than U.S. livestock, and does not meet its objective to provide complete information to consumers on the origin of meat products. In March 2012, the United States appealed the WTO ruling. In June 2012 the WTO's Appellate Body (AB) upheld the DS panel's finding that COOL treats imported livestock less favorably than domestic livestock. But the AB reversed the finding that COOL does not fulfill its legitimate objective to provide consumers with information on origin. The United States welcomed the AB's affirmation of

the right to adopt labeling requirements to inform consumers on the origin of their meat. Participants in the U.S. livestock sector had mixed reactions, reflecting the ongoing heated debate on COOL. Bills: P.L. 107-171, P.L. 110-246, H.R. 2393, S. 1844, H.R. 22, P.L. 109-97, P.L. 113-235, H.R. 2642. Order No. RS22955.

LEGAL ISSUES WITH FEDERAL LABELING OF GENETICALLY ENGINEERED FOOD: IN BRIEF, by Emily M. Lanza, Legislative Attorney. 13 pages. Updated March 11, 2016. Genetically engineered (GE) foods, sometimes referred to as genetically modified foods (GMO foods), are foods that are derived from scientific methods used to introduce new traits or characteristics to an organism. The labeling of GE foods has been the subject of debate among members of the general public and federal and state governments since the introduction of GE foods to the food supply in the 1990s. Federal law does not impose specific labeling requirements on a food just because it may or may not contain GE ingredients or was derived using GE techniques. The Food and Drug Administration (FDA) has yet to issue formal regulations and policies on the labeling of GE food. However, this absence of direct federal regulation does not mean that GE foods are free from any federal oversight. Instead, labels of GE foods follow the same federal labeling requirements and guidelines outlined in the Federal Food, Drug, and Cosmetic Act (FFDCA) as non-GE foods. These labeling requirements prohibit false or misleading labels and address material information that may be relevant to the consumption of that food. However, some states have enacted laws that specifically demand manufacturers disclose the presence of GE ingredients in certain foods on the label. The United States Department of Agriculture's (USDA's) oversight over organic meat and poultry products involves the regulation of GE ingredients. However, the discussion of such oversight is beyond the scope of this report. Bills:

H.R. 913, H.R. 1599, S. 511, S. 2621. Order No. R43705

SCHOOL MEALS PROGRAMS AND OTHER USDA CHILD NUTRITION PROGRAMS: A PRIMER, by Randy Alison Aussenberg, Specialist in Nutrition Assistance Policy. 43 pages. Updated March 15, 2016. This report presents an overview of the benefits and services these programs and related activities provide as well as participation and funding information. The report emphasizes details for the school meals programs and provides an orientation to the operations of the other programs. Bills: H.R. 1728, H.R. 2715, S. 1539, S. 613, S. 1966. Order No. R43783.

FOREIGN AID

U.S. FOREIGN AID TO THE PALESTINIANS, by Jim Zanotti, Specialist in Middle Eastern Affairs. 27 pages. Updated March 18, 2016. Since June 2007, these U.S. policy priorities have crystallized around the factional and geographical split between the Fatah-led Palestinian Authority (PA) in the West Bank and Hamas in the Gaza Strip. From FY2008 to the present, annual Economic Support Fund (ESF) assistance to the West Bank and Gaza Strip has averaged around $400 million, with that amount divided between U.S. Agency for International Development (USAID)-administered project assistance (through grants and contracts) and budget support for the Palestinian Authority (PA). Annual International Narcotics Control and Law Enforcement (INCLE) non-lethal assistance for PA security forces and the criminal justice sector in the West Bank has averaged around $100 million. In line with Obama Administration requests, baseline funding levels for both ESF (including ESF-Overseas Contingency Operations, or ESF-OCO) and INCLE have declined since FY2013, with FY2017 requested annual assistance amounts of $327.6 million for ESF and $35 million for INCLE. Because of congressional concerns that, among other things,

U.S. aid to the Palestinians might be diverted to Palestinian terrorist groups, the aid is subject to a host of vetting and oversight requirements and legislative restrictions. Additionally, the United States is the largest single-state donor to the U.N. Relief and Works Agency for Palestine Refugees in the Near East (UNRWA). Bills: H.R. 4522, H.R. 3829, S. 2537. Order No. RS22967.

FOREIGN COUNTRIES & REGIONS

IRAN NUCLEAR AGREEMENT, by Kenneth Katzman, Specialist in Middle Eastern Affairs; Paul K. Kerr, Analyst in Nonproliferation. 39 pages. Updated March 7, 2016. On July 14, 2015, Iran and the six powers that have negotiated with Iran about its nuclear program since 2006 (the United States, the United Kingdom, France, Russia, China, and Germany-collectively known as the P5+1) finalized a Joint Comprehensive Plan of Action (JCPOA). The JCPOA is intended to ensure that Iran's nuclear program can be used for purely peaceful purposes, in exchange for a broad lifting of U.S., European Union (EU), and United Nations (U.N.) sanctions on Iran. The JCPOA largely reflects what was agreed in an April 2, 2015, framework for the accord. The agreement replaces a Joint Plan of Action (JPA) interim nuclear accord in operation since January 2014. The Administration and the other P5+1 governments assert that the JCPOA represents the most effective means to ensure that Iran cannot obtain a nuclear weapon, and that all U.S. options to prevent Iran from developing a nuclear weapon remain available even after the key nuclear restrictions of the JCPOA expire. The Administration further asserts that the JCPOA contains provisions for U.N. sanctions to be reimposed if Iran is found not in compliance with its requirements, although the Administration and many experts acknowledge it is difficult to predict the degree to which international governments might reimpose their sanctions. Bills: H.R. 3461, H.R. 3460, H.R. 3646, S. 2094, H.R. 3273, H.R. 3457, S. 2086, H.R. 3728, H.R. 3662. Order No. R43333

ISRAEL: BACKGROUND AND U.S. RELATIONS IN BRIEF, by Jim Zanotti, Specialist in Middle Eastern Affairs. 16 pages. Updated March 16, 2016. The longtime U.S. commitment to Israel's security and "qualitative military edge" in the region is intended to enable Israel to defend itself against threats it perceives, which in recent years have largely come from Iran and groups Iran supports-such as Hezbollah in Lebanon and Hamas in the West Bank and Gaza Strip. The political complement to this cooperation has been a long-standing U.S. effort to encourage Israel and other regional actors to improve relations with one another. U.S. policymakers have sponsored or mediated numerous Arab-Israeli peace initiatives since the 1970s, including Israel's peace treaties with Egypt and Jordan and interim agreements with the Palestine Liberation Organization (PLO). However, largely owing to lingering Israeli-Palestinian disputes and widespread Middle Eastern turmoil, the objective of formal political normalization for Israel within the region has eluded successive Administrations. Order No. R44245.

LATIN AMERICA AND THE CARIBBEAN: FACT SHEET ON LEADERS AND ELECTIONS, by Anne Leland, Information Research Specialist. 4 pages. Updated March 1, 2016. This report provides the results of recent elections in Latin America and the Caribbean. Below are three tables organized by region, including the date of each country's independence, the name of the newly elected president or prime minister, and the projected date of the next election. Information in this report was gathered from numerous sources, including the U.S. State Department, Central Intelligence Agency's (CIA's) World Fact Book, International Foundation for Electoral Systems (IFES) Election Guide, Economist Intelligence Unit (EIU), and other news sources. Order No. 98-684.

TURKEY: BACKGROUND AND U.S. RELATIONS IN BRIEF, by Jim Zanotti, Specialist in Middle Eastern Affairs. 17 pages. Updated March 18, 2016. Several Turkish foreign and domestic policy issues have significant relevance for U.S. interests, and Congress plays an active role in shaping and overseeing U.S. relations with Turkey. This report provides information and analysis relevant for Congress on the following: - Assessments of U.S.-Turkey relations and Turkish foreign policy. - Various aspects of U.S.-Turkey cooperation against the Islamic State organization (IS, also known as Daesh, ISIS, and ISIL) in Syria and Iraq, including border security and discussion of "safe zones," foreign fighters and smuggling, refugees, and complications regarding Kurdish groups. - Turkey's November 24, 2015, downing of a Russian aircraft and a possible improvement of Turkey-Israel ties. - Key issues regarding Turkey's domestic politics. These include controversies and questions involving Turkey's President Recep Tayyip Erdogan and the ruling Justice and Development Party (Adalet ve Kalkinma Partisi or AKP) following the AKP's November 2015 electoral victory, and the Turkish government's renewed hostilities (since July) with the longtime Kurdish nationalist insurgent group PKK (Kurdistan Workers' Party or Partiya Karkeren Kurdistan). Order No. R44000.

U.S.-EU COOPERATION AGAINST TERRORISM, by Kristin Archick, Specialist in European Affairs. 35 pages. Updated March 2, 2016. Congressional decisions related to data privacy, intelligence-gathering, border controls, visa policy, and transport security may affect how future U.S.-EU counterterrorism cooperation evolves. EU officials have welcomed passage of the Judicial Redress Act (P.L. 114-126) to provide EU citizens with a limited right of judicial redress for privacy violations in a law enforcement context, but they have expressed unease with some provisions in the Visa Waiver Program Improvement and Terrorist Travel Prevention Act of 2015 (passed as part of P.L.

114-113 in the wake of the Paris attacks and heightened U.S. concerns about European citizens fighting with terrorist groups abroad). Given the European Parliament's growing influence in many of these policy areas, Members of Congress may be able to help shape the Parliament's views and responses through ongoing contacts and the existing Transatlantic Legislators' Dialogue (TLD). This report examines the evolution of U.S.-EU counterterrorism cooperation, current issues, and the ongoing challenges that may be of interest in the 114th Congress. Also see CRS Report R44003, European Fighters in Syria and Iraq: Assessments, Responses, and Issues for the United States, coordinated by Kristin Archick. Bills: H.R. 1428, 4830, S. 1600. Order No. RS22030.

GENERAL INTEREST

DAYLIGHT SAVING TIME, by Beth Cook, Information Research Specialist. 9 pages. March 9, 2016. Daylight Saving Time (DST) is a period of the year between spring and fall when clocks in the United States are set one hour ahead of standard time. DST is currently observed in the United States from 2:00 a.m. on the second Sunday in March until 2:00 a.m. on the first Sunday in November. The following states and territories do not observe DST: Arizona (except the Navajo Nation, which does observe DST), Hawaii, American Samoa, Guam, the Northern Mariana Islands, Puerto Rico, and the Virgin Islands. Order No. R44411.

RESOURCES FOR GRANTSEEKERS, by Merete F. Gerli, Information Research Specialist. 10 pages. Updated March 21, 2016. This report describes key sources of information on government and private funding, and outlines eligibility for federal grants. Federal grants are intended for projects benefiting states and communities. Individuals may be eligible for other kinds of benefits or assistance, or small businesses and students may be eligible for loans. Free information is readily available to grant

seekers, who generally know best the details of their projects. The Catalog of Federal Domestic Assistance (CFDA) describes more than 2,200 federal programs, more than half of them grants, and can be searched by keyword, subject, department or agency, program title, beneficiary, and applicant eligibility. Federal department and agency websites provide additional information and guidance, and they provide state agency contacts. Once a program has been identified, eligible grant seekers may apply electronically for grants at the website Grants.gov through a uniform process for all agencies. Through Grants.gov, grant seekers may identify when federal funding notices and deadlines for a CFDA program become available, sign up for e-mail notification of funding opportunities, and track the progress of submitted applications. Order No. RL34012.

GOVERNMENT EMPLOYEES

THE FEDERAL EMPLOYEES' COMPENSATION ACT (FECA): WORKERS' COMPENSATION FOR FEDERAL EMPLOYEES, by Scott Szymendera, Analyst in Disability Policy. 25 pages. Updated March 18, 2016. The Federal Employees' Compensation Act (FECA) is the workers' compensation program for federal employees. Like all workers' compensation programs, FECA pays disability, survivors, and medical benefits, without fault, to employees who are injured or become ill in the course of their federal employment and the survivors of employees killed on the job. The FECA program is administered by the Department of Labor (DOL) and the costs of benefits are paid by each employee's host agency. Employees of the U.S. Postal Service (USPS) currently comprise the largest group of FECA beneficiaries and are responsible for the largest share of FECA benefits. Bills: H.R. 2309, H.R. 2465, H.R. 1196, H.R. 15316, H.R. 3141, H.R. 3191, H.R. 12383, H.R. 10721, H.R. 13871. Order No. R42107.

GOVERNMENT INFORMATION

ACCESS TO GOVERNMENT INFORMATION IN THE UNITED STATES: A PRIMER, by Wendy Ginsberg, Analyst in Government Organization and Management. 9 pages. Updated March 18, 2016. This report offers an introduction to the four access laws and provides citations to additional resources related to these statutes. This report includes statistics on the use of FOIA and FACA and on litigation related to FOIA. The 113th Congress may have an interest in overseeing the implementation of these laws or may consider amending the laws. In addition, this report provides some examples of the methods Congress, the President, and the Courts have employed to provide or require the provision of information to one another. This report is a primer on information access in the U.S. federal government and provides a list of resources related to transparency, secrecy, access, and nondisclosure. Order No. 97-71.

DAYLIGHT SAVING TIME, by Beth Cook, Information Research Specialist. 9 pages. March 9, 2016. Daylight Saving Time (DST) is a period of the year between spring and fall when clocks in the United States are set one hour ahead of standard time. DST is currently observed in the United States from 2:00 a.m. on the second Sunday in March until 2:00 a.m. on the first Sunday in November. The following states and territories do not observe DST: Arizona (except the Navajo Nation, which does observe DST), Hawaii, American Samoa, Guam, the Northern Mariana Islands, Puerto Rico, and the Virgin Islands. Order No. R44411.

RESOURCES FOR GRANTSEEKERS, by Merete F. Gerli, Information Research Specialist. 10 pages. Updated March 21, 2016. This report describes key sources of information on government and private funding, and outlines eligibility for federal grants. Federal grants are intended for projects benefiting states and communities. Individuals may be eligible for other kinds of benefits or assistance, or small businesses and students may be eligible for loans. Free information is readily available to grant seekers, who generally know best the details of their projects. The Catalog of Federal Domestic Assistance (CFDA) describes more than 2,200 federal programs, more than half of them grants, and can be searched by keyword, subject, department or agency, program title, beneficiary, and applicant eligibility. Federal department and agency websites provide additional information and guidance, and they provide state agency contacts. Once a program has been identified, eligible grant seekers may apply electronically for grants at the website Grants.gov through a uniform process for all agencies. Through Grants.gov, grant seekers may identify when federal funding notices and deadlines for a CFDA program become available, sign up for e-mail notification of funding opportunities, and track the progress of submitted applications. Order No. RL34012.

HEALTH POLICY

CONSUMER OPERATED AND ORIENTED PLAN (CO-OP) PROGRAM: FREQUENTLY ASKED QUESTIONS, by Annie L. Mach, Analyst in Health Care Financing; Grant A. Driessen, Analyst in Public Finance. 16 pages. March 11, 2016. The Consumer Operated and Oriented Plan (CO-OP) program was included in the Patient Protection and Affordable Care Act (ACA; P.L. 111-148) in an effort to increase the competitiveness of state health insurance markets and improve choice. Under the program, the Centers for Medicare & Medicaid Services (CMS) uses appropriated funds to award low-interest loans to organizations applying to become CO-OPs-nonprofit, member-run health insurance issuers that sell health insurance in the state(s) in which they are licensed. Order No. R44414.

ELIGIBILITY AND DETERMINATION OF HEALTH INSURANCE PREMIUM TAX

CREDITS AND COST-SHARING SUBSIDIES: IN BRIEF, by Bernadette Fernandez, Specialist in Health Care Financing. 14 pages. March 23, 2016. Certain individuals without access to subsidized health insurance coverage may be eligible for premium tax credits, as established under the Patient Protection and Affordable Care Act (ACA; P.L. 111-148, as amended). The dollar amount of the premium credit varies from individual to individual, based on a formula specified in statute. Individuals who are eligible for the premium credit, however, generally are still required to contribute some amount toward the purchase of health insurance. Order No. R44425.

EXCISE TAX ON HIGH-COST EMPLOYER-SPONSORED HEALTH COVERAGE: IN BRIEF, by Annie L. Mach, Analyst in Health Care Financing. 11 pages. Updated March 24, 2016. The Patient Protection and Affordable Care Act (ACA; P.L. 111-148, as amended) includes a 40% excise tax on employer-sponsored health coverage. This tax, often called the Cadillac tax, is to be implemented beginning in 2018. The excise tax was included in the ACA to raise revenue to offset the cost of other ACA provisions. According to the Congressional Budget Office and the Joint Committee on Taxation, the excise tax is expected to increase federal revenues by $87 billion between 2016 and 2025. The excise tax applies to the aggregate cost of an employee's applicable coverage that exceeds a dollar limit. Applicable coverage includes, but is not limited to, the employer's and the employee's contribution to health insurance premiums and certain contributions to tax-advantaged health accounts (e.g., health care flexible spending accounts, or FSAs). Order No. R44147.

MEDICARE PRIMER, by Patricia A. Davis, Coordinator, Specialist in Health Care Financing. 40 pages. Updated March 21, 2016. This report provides a general overview of the Medicare program including descriptions of the program's history, eligibility criteria, covered services, provider payment systems, and program administration and financing. A list of commonly used acronyms, as well as information on beneficiary cost sharing, may be found in the appendixes. Order No. R40425.

MEDICARE: PART B PREMIUMS, by Patricia A. Davis, Specialist in Health Care Financing. 48 pages. Updated March 25, 2016. Medicare is a federal insurance program that pays for covered health care services of most individuals aged 65 and older and certain disabled persons. In 2016, the program is expected to cover about 57 million persons (48 million aged and 9 million disabled) at a total cost of $688 billion. Most individuals (or their spouses) aged 65 and older who have worked in covered employment and paid Medicare payroll taxes for 40 quarters receive premium-free Medicare Part A (Hospital Insurance). Those entitled to Medicare Part A (regardless of whether they are eligible for premium-free Part A) have the option of enrolling in Part B, which covers such things as physician and outpatient services and medical equipment. Bills: H.R. 1418, H.R. 1314, H.R. 2, H.R. 3696, H.R. 4090, H.R. 2476, H.R. 1654, H.R. 2235, S. 1453, S. 1961. Order No. R40082

PRESCRIPTION DRUG MONITORING PROGRAMS, by Kristin M. Finklea, Specialist in Domestic Security; Erin Bagalman, Analyst in Health Policy; Lisa N. Sacco, Analyst in Illicit Drugs and Crime Policy. 28 pages. Updated March 23, 2016. This report provides an overview of PDMPs, including their operation, enforcement mechanisms, costs, and financing. It also examines the effectiveness of PDMPs and outlines federal grants supporting PDMPs. Finally, this report discusses relevant considerations for policymakers including interstate data sharing, interoperability, protection of health information, and the possible link between the crackdown on prescription drug abuse and rise in heroin abuse. Bills: H.R. 1725,

H.R. 866, H.R. 3528, H.R. 1725, S. 2529, S. 480. Order No. R42593.

HEALTH CARE FOR DEPENDENTS AND SURVIVORS OF VETERANS, by Sidath Viranga Panangala, Specialist in Veterans Policy. 18 pages. Updated March 3, 2016. The Civilian Health and Medical Program of the Department of Veterans Affairs (CHAMPVA) was established by the Veterans' Health Care Expansion Act of 1973 (P.L. 93-82). CHAMPVA is primarily a health insurance program where certain eligible dependents and survivors of veterans receive care from private sector health care providers. Bills: H.R. 9048, H.R. 5136, H.R. 6523, H.R. 115, H.R. 288, H.R. 218, S. 490, S. 325, S. 170. Order No. RS22483.

IMPROVING CHILD NUTRITION INTEGRITY AND ACCESS ACT OF 2016: IN BRIEF, by Randy Alison Aussenberg, Specialist in Nutrition Assistance Policy. 11 pages. Updated March 15, 2016. This report offers some basic background on the last reauthorization, its expiration, and some of the policies in the Senate committee's legislation. Please see the Senate committee's resources for further details on the committee print and the legislative text.
Bills: H.R. 1728, H.R. 2715, S. 1539, S. 1966. Order No. R44373.

OLDER AMERICANS ACT: BACKGROUND AND OVERVIEW, by Kirsten J. Colello, Specialist in Health and Aging Policy; Angela Napili, Information Research Specialist. 25 pages. Updated March 15, 2016. This report first provides information on the OAA's historical development. Next, it briefly describes the act's titles, highlighting selected provisions. Bills: H.R. 3850, H.R. 4122, H.R. 2029, S. 192, S. 1028, S. 1562. Order No. R43414.

PATIENT PROTECTION AND AFFORDABLE CARE ACT (ACA):

RESOURCES FOR FREQUENTLY ASKED QUESTIONS, by Angela Napili, Information Research Specialist. 28 pages. Updated March 3, 2016. This report provides resources to help congressional staff respond to constituents' frequently asked questions (FAQs) about the Patient Protection and Affordable Care Act (ACA; P.L. 111-148, as amended). The report lists selected resources regarding consumers, employers, and other stakeholders, with a focus on federal sources. It also lists Congressional Research Service (CRS) reports that summarize the ACA's provisions. The resources are arranged by topic. This list is not a comprehensive directory of all resources on the ACA but rather is intended to address a few questions that may arise frequently. Order No. R43215

THE AGENCY FOR HEALTHCARE RESEARCH AND QUALITY (AHRQ) BUDGET: FACT SHEET, by Amanda K. Sarata, Specialist in Health Policy. 5 pages. Updated March 15, 2016. The AHRQ budget has traditionally been organized into the program areas of Health Costs, Quality, and Outcomes (HCQO) Research; MEPS; and program support. As of FY2017, HCQO focuses on four priority areas, including (1) Health Information Technology Research; (2) Patient Safety; (3) Health Services Research, Data and Dissemination; and (4) U.S. Preventive Services Task Force. For several years, HCQO included a patient-centered health research (comparative effectiveness research) area, but this area was first removed in the FY2016 congressional budget justification and the FY2016 President's budget request, and continued to be excluded in FY2017 documents. In addition, HCQO had previously included a "Value" category, but that area was removed in the FY2017 President's budget request and in the FY2017 congressional budget justification. Order No. R44136/

TITLE X (PUBLIC HEALTH SERVICE ACT) FAMILY PLANNING PROGRAM, by Angela Napili, Information Research Specialist.

22 pages. Updated March 15, 2016. The federal government provides grants for voluntary family planning services through the Family Planning Program, Title X of the Public Health Service Act (42 U.S.C. §§300 to 300a-6). Enacted in 1970, it is the only domestic federal program devoted solely to family planning and related preventive health services. In 2014, Title X-funded clinics served 4.1 million clients. Title X is administered through the Office of Population Affairs (OPA) in the Department of Health and Human Services (HHS). Although the authorization of appropriations for Title X ended with FY1985, funding for the program has continued through appropriations bills for the Departments of Labor, Health and Human Services, and Education, and Related Agencies (Labor-HHS-Education). The FY2015 Consolidated and Further Continuing Appropriations Act (P.L. 113-235) provided $286 million for Title X, the same as the FY2014 level. The FY2015 act continued previous years' requirements that Title X funds not be spent on abortions, that all pregnancy counseling be nondirective, and that funds not be spent on promoting or opposing any legislative proposal or candidate for public office. Grantees continued to be required to certify that they encourage "family participation" when minors seek family planning services and to certify that they counsel minors on how to resist attempted coercion into sexual activity. The appropriations law also clarified that family planning providers are not exempt from state notification and reporting laws on child abuse, child molestation, sexual abuse, rape, or incest. Bills: H.R. 2764, H.R. 1105. Order No. RL33644.

HOUSING

DEPARTMENT OF HOUSING AND URBAN DEVELOPMENT (HUD): FUNDING TRENDS SINCE FY2002, by Maggie McCarty, Specialist in Housing Policy. 19 pages. Updated March 17, 2016. This report explores the trends in HUD's funding since FY2002. It begins with an explanation of the key budget concepts necessary to understand those trends. It concludes with a discussion of factors that may influence HUD's budget going forward. Order No. R42542.

FHA-INSURED HOME LOANS: AN OVERVIEW, by Katie Jones, Analyst in Housing Policy. 20 pages. Updated March 16, 2016. This report provides background on FHA's history and market role and an overview of the basic eligibility and underwriting criteria for FHA-insured home loans. It also provides data on the number and dollar volume of mortgages that FHA insures, along with data on FHA's market share in recent years. It does not go into detail on the financial status of the FHA mortgage insurance fund; for information on FHA's financial position, see CRS Report R42875, FHA Single-Family Mortgage Insurance: Financial Status of the Mutual Mortgage Insurance Fund (MMI Fund), by Katie Jones. Recent FHA policy changes are discussed in CRS Report R43531, FHA Single- Family Mortgage Insurance: Recent Policy Changes and Proposed Legislation, by Katie Jones. Order No. RS20530.

HOUSING ISSUES IN THE 114TH CONGRESS, by Katie Jones, Coordinator Analyst in Housing Policy; David H. Carpenter Legislative Attorney. 41 pages. Updated March 3, 2016.
This report begins with an overview of housing and mortgage market conditions to provide context for the housing issues that Congress has been considering, and then discusses major housing issues active in the 114th Congress. This report is meant to provide a broad overview of the issues and is not intended to provide detailed information or analysis. However, it includes references to other, more in-depth CRS reports on the issues where possible. Bills: H.R. 233, H.R. 2482, H.R. 3700, H.R. 360, H.R. 574, H.R. 2577, H.R. 22, H.R. 650, H.R. 685, H.R. 3145, H.R. 2578, H.R. 2577, H.R. 2029, H.R. 4479, S. 710, S. 1484, S. 1910. Order No. R44304.

HOUSING OPPORTUNITY THROUGH MODERNIZATION ACT OF 2015 (H.R. 3700): IN BRIEF, by Maggie McCarty, Specialist in Housing Policy; Libby Perl, Specialist in Housing Policy; Katie Jones, Analyst in Housing Policy. 18 pages. Updated March 3, 2016. The Housing Opportunity Through Modernization Act of 2015 (H.R. 3700), as ordered reported by the House Financial Services Committee on December 9, 2015, includes modifications to a number of federal housing programs, mostly administered by the Department of Housing and Urban Development (HUD). Many of the changes proposed in the bill have been considered by prior Congresses in some version as a part of broader assisted housing reform legislation. Some provisions in the bill have been introduced in the 114th Congress in other bills, some were requested in the President's budget, and others are new. Bills: H.R. 3700, H.R. 1047, H.R. 251. Order No. R44358.

SECTION 202 AND OTHER HUD RENTAL HOUSING PROGRAMS FOR LOW-INCOME ELDERLY RESIDENTS, by Libby Perl, Specialist in Housing Policy. 30 pages. Updated March 7, 2016. This report provides a summary of the HUD programs that provide multi-family rental housing for low-income elderly households and their related supportive services programs. It also discusses funding and current issues in the area of assisted housing for low-income elderly persons. However, the report does not include a comprehensive look at all housing programs that serve elderly households. Major sources of assistance that are not discussed include HUD's Section 8 voucher program,7 HUD's mortgage insurance and reverse mortgage programs,8 and the Department of Agriculture's rural housing programs that provide assistance to elderly households. Bills: H.R. 8, H.R. 5, H.R. 3, H.R. 31, S. 566. Order No. RL33508.

SECTION 811 AND OTHER HUD HOUSING PROGRAMS FOR PERSONS WITH DISABILITIES, by Libby Perl, Specialist in Housing Policy. 36 pages. Updated March 7, 2016. This report describes how federal funds are used to develop housing designated for persons with disabilities. It also discusses recent funding for the Section 811 program and current issues surrounding housing for persons with disabilities, including mixed financing arrangements, worst case housing needs, and persons with disabilities who are homeless. Bills: H.R. 12433, H.R. 4, H.R. 5576, H.R. 1158, S. 3084. Order No. RL34728.

HUMANITIES

THE CORPORATION FOR PUBLIC BROADCASTING: FEDERAL FUNDING AND ISSUES, by Glenn J. McLoughlin, Section Research Manager; Rita Tehan, Information Research Specialist. 12 pages. Updated March 8, 2016. The Corporation for Public Broadcasting (CPB) receives virtually all of its funding through federal appropriations; overall, about 15% of public television and 10% of radio broadcasting funding comes from the federal appropriations that CPB distributes. CPB's appropriation is allocated through a distribution formula established in its authorizing legislation and has historically received two-year advanced appropriations. Congressional policy makers are increasingly interested in the federal role in supporting CPB due to concerns over the federal debt, the role of the federal government funding for public radio and television, and whether public broadcasting provides a balanced and nuanced approach to covering news of national interest. It is also important to note that many congressional policy makers defend the federal role of funding public broadcasting. They contend that it provides news and information to large segments of the population that seek to understand complex policy issues in depth, and in particular for children's television broadcasting, has a significant and positive impact on early learning and education for children. Order No. RS22168.

IMMIGRATION

ELECTRONIC EMPLOYMENT ELIGIBILITY VERIFICATION, by Andorra Bruno, Specialist in Immigration Policy. 22 pages. Updated March 23, 2016. Unauthorized immigration and unauthorized employment continue to be key issues in the ongoing debate over immigration policy. Today's discussions about these issues build on the work of prior Congresses. In 1986, following many years of debate about unauthorized immigration to the United States; Congress passed the Immigration Reform and Control Act (IRCA). This law sought to address unauthorized immigration, in part, by requiring all employers to examine documents presented by new hires to verify identity and work authorization and to complete and retain employment eligibility verification (I-9) forms. Ten years later, in the face of a growing unauthorized population, Congress attempted to strengthen the employment verification process by establishing pilot programs for electronic verification, as part of the Illegal Immigration Reform and Immigrant Responsibility Act of 1996 (IIRIRA).

The Basic Pilot program (known now as E-Verify), the first of the three IIRIRA employment verification pilots to be implemented and the only one still in operation, began in November 1997. Originally scheduled to terminate in November 2001, it has been extended several times. It is currently authorized until September 30, 2016, in accordance with the Consolidated Appropriations Act, 2016 (P.L. 114-113). Bills: H.R. 1772, S. 744. Order No. R40446

ALIENS' RIGHT TO COUNSEL IN REMOVAL PROCEEDINGS: IN BRIEF, by Kate M. Manuel, Legislative Attorney. 14 pages. Updated March 17, 2016. This report provides an overview of the various legal authorities governing aliens' right to counsel-as that term is broadly understood-in removal proceedings. It does not address aliens' right to counsel in criminal proceedings, the outcomes of which could potentially affect their ability to remain in the United States under immigration law. The report also does not address effective assistance of counsel. Order No. R43613

INTERNATIONAL AFFAIRS

IRAN NUCLEAR AGREEMENT, by Kenneth Katzman, Specialist in Middle Eastern Affairs; Paul K. Kerr, Analyst in Nonproliferation. 39 pages. Updated March 7, 2016. On July 14, 2015, Iran and the six powers that have negotiated with Iran about its nuclear program since 2006 (the United States, the United Kingdom, France, Russia, China, and Germany-collectively known as the P5+1) finalized a Joint Comprehensive Plan of Action (JCPOA). The JCPOA is intended to ensure that Iran's nuclear program can be used for purely peaceful purposes, in exchange for a broad lifting of U.S., European Union (EU), and United Nations (U.N.) sanctions on Iran. The JCPOA largely reflects what was agreed in an April 2, 2015, framework for the accord. The agreement replaces a Joint Plan of Action (JPA) interim nuclear accord in operation since January 2014. The Administration and the other P5+1 governments assert that the JCPOA represents the most effective means to ensure that Iran cannot obtain a nuclear weapon, and that all U.S. options to prevent Iran from developing a nuclear weapon remain available even after the key nuclear restrictions of the JCPOA expire. The Administration further asserts that the JCPOA contains provisions for U.N. sanctions to be reimposed if Iran is found not in compliance with its requirements, although the Administration and many experts acknowledge it is difficult to predict the degree to which international governments might reimpose their sanctions. Bills: H.R. 3461, H.R. 3460, H.R. 3646, S. 2094, H.R. 3273, H.R. 3457, S. 2086, H.R. 3728, H.R. 3662. Order No. R43333

INTERNATIONAL FINANCE

FOREIGN CORRUPT PRACTICES ACT (FCPA): CONGRESSIONAL INTEREST AND EXECUTIVE ENFORCEMENT, by Michael V. Seitzinger, Legislative Attorney. 11 pages. Updated March 15, 2016. During the mid-1970s investigations and administrative and legal actions against numerous domestic corporations revealed that the practice of making questionable or illegal payments by United States corporations to foreign government officials existed to some extent within the American business community.1 The legal and regulatory mechanisms for dealing with these payments had involved actions by the Securities and Exchange Commission (SEC) against public corporations for concealing from required public disclosure substantial payments made by the firm, including to foreign government officials. There was also the potential for an antitrust action for restraints of trade or fraud prosecutions by the Department of Justice (DOJ). Government officials and administrators contended that more direct prohibitions on foreign bribery and more detailed requirements concerning corporate recordkeeping and accountability were needed to deal effectively with the problem. The revelations of slush funds and secret payments by American corporations were stated to have affected adversely American foreign policy, damaged abroad the image of American democracy, and impaired public confidence in the financial integrity of American corporations. Bills: H.R. 616, H.R. 5366, H.R. 5837, H.R. 2152, H.R. 3531, H.R. 3588, H.R. 4178. Order No. R41466

INTERNATIONAL TRADE AND FINANCE: KEY POLICY ISSUES FOR THE 114TH CONGRESS, by Mary A. Irace, Coordinator Section Research Manager; Brock R. Williams, Coordinator Analyst in International Trade and Finance. 38 pages. Updated February 29, 2016. Congress is in a unique position to address these issues, particularly given its constitutional authority for legislating and overseeing international trade and financial policy. This report provides a brief overview of some of the trade and finance issues that may come before the second session of the 114th Congress. Appendix A provides a list of CRS products covering these issues in greater detail. Bills: H.R. 1191, H.R. 2297, H.R. 757, H.R. 3662, H.R. 644, S. 284, S. 433. Order No. R43841.

LABOR

ELECTRONIC EMPLOYMENT ELIGIBILITY VERIFICATION, by Andorra Bruno, Specialist in Immigration Policy. 22 pages. Updated March 23, 2016. Unauthorized immigration and unauthorized employment continue to be key issues in the ongoing debate over immigration policy. Today's discussions about these issues build on the work of prior Congresses. In 1986, following many years of debate about unauthorized immigration to the United States; Congress passed the Immigration Reform and Control Act (IRCA). This law sought to address unauthorized immigration, in part, by requiring all employers to examine documents presented by new hires to verify identity and work authorization and to complete and retain employment eligibility verification (I-9) forms. Ten years later, in the face of a growing unauthorized population, Congress attempted to strengthen the employment verification process by establishing pilot programs for electronic verification, as part of the Illegal Immigration Reform and Immigrant Responsibility Act of 1996 (IIRIRA). The Basic Pilot program (known now as E-Verify), the first of the three IIRIRA employment verification pilots to be implemented and the only one still in operation, began in November 1997. Originally scheduled to terminate in November 2001, it has been extended several times. It is currently authorized until September 30, 2016, in accordance with the Consolidated Appropriations Act, 2016 (P.L. 114-113). Bills: H.R. 1772, S. 744. Order No. R40446

UNEMPLOYMENT INSURANCE: LEGISLATIVE ISSUES IN THE 114TH

CONGRESS, by Julie M. Whittaker, Specialist in Income Security; Katelin P. Isaacs, Analyst in Income Security. 15 pages. Updated March 23, 2016. This report describes proposed UI legislation in the 114th Congress, organized by the following categories: Concurrent receipt of Social Security Disability Insurance (SSDI) and UI benefits-S. 343, S. 499, and H.R. 918 UI program integrity-H.R. 2503 and H.R. 2512 Unemployment Compensation for Former Service members (UCX)-S. 1376 Drug testing-H.R. 1136 and H.R. 2148 Rehiring UI Beneficiaries and Exhaustees-H.R. 481 and H.R. 2265 Vouchers and Demonstration Projects-H.R. 2509 Job Training and Education-H.R. 2219. Bills: H.R. 918, H.R. 2503, H.R. 2512, H.R. 1735, H.R. 1136, H.R. 2148, H.R. 2512, H.R. 481, H.R. 2265, H.R. 2721, H.R. 3555, S. 2005, S. 1517. Order No. R43993.

SMALL BUSINESS ADMINISTRATION AND JOB CREATION, by Robert Jay Dilger, Senior Specialist in American National Government. 22 pages. Updated March 8, 2016. This report examines the economic research on net job creation to identify the types of businesses that appear to create the most jobs. That research suggests that business startups play an important role in job creation, but have a more limited effect on net job creation over time because fewer than half of all startups are still in business after five years. However, the influence of small business startups on net job creation varies by firm size. Startups with fewer than 20 employees tend to have a negligible effect on net job creation over time whereas startups with 20-499 employees tend to have a positive employment effect, as do surviving younger businesses of all sizes (in operation for one year to five years). This report then examines the possible implications this research might have for Congress and the SBA. For example, the SBA provides assistance to all qualifying businesses that meet its size standards. About 97% of all businesses currently meet the SBA's eligibility criteria. Given congressional interest in job

creation, this report examines the potential consequences of targeting small business assistance to a narrower group, small businesses that are the most likely to create and retain the most jobs. This report also examines the arguments for providing federal assistance to small businesses, noting that policy makers often view job creation as a justification for such assistance whereas economists argue that over the long term federal assistance to small businesses is likely to reallocate jobs within the economy, not increase them. Nonetheless, most economists support federal assistance to small businesses for other purposes, such as a means to correct a perceived market failure related to the disadvantages small businesses experience when attempting to access capital and credit. Order No. R41523.

THE FEDERAL EMPLOYEES' COMPENSATION ACT (FECA): WORKERS' COMPENSATION FOR FEDERAL EMPLOYEES, by Scott Szymendera, Analyst in Disability Policy. 25 pages. Updated March 18, 2016. The Federal Employees' Compensation Act (FECA) is the workers' compensation program for federal employees. Like all workers' compensation programs, FECA pays disability, survivors, and medical benefits, without fault, to employees who are injured or become ill in the course of their federal employment and the survivors of employees killed on the job. The FECA program is administered by the Department of Labor (DOL) and the costs of benefits are paid by each employee's host agency. Employees of the U.S. Postal Service (USPS) currently comprise the largest group of FECA beneficiaries and are responsible for the largest share of FECA benefits. Bills: H.R. 2309, H.R. 2465, H.R. 1196, H.R. 15316, H.R. 3141, H.R. 3191, H.R. 12383, H.R. 10721, H.R. 13871. Order No. R42107.

MEDICINE

PRESCRIPTION DRUG MONITORING PROGRAMS, by Kristin M. Finklea, Specialist in Domestic Security; Erin Bagalman, Analyst in Health Policy; Lisa N. Sacco, Analyst in Illicit Drugs and Crime Policy. 28 pages. Updated March 23, 2016. This report provides an overview of PDMPs, including their operation, enforcement mechanisms, costs, and financing. It also examines the effectiveness of PDMPs and outlines federal grants supporting PDMPs. Finally, this report discusses relevant considerations for policymakers including interstate data sharing, interoperability, protection of health information, and the possible link between the crackdown on prescription drug abuse and rise in heroin abuse. Bills: H.R. 1725, H.R. 866, H.R. 3528, H.R. 1725, S. 2529, S. 480. Order No. R42593.

NATURAL RESOURCES

NUTRIENTS IN AGRICULTURAL PRODUCTION: A WATER QUALITY OVERVIEW, by Megan Stubbs, Specialist in Agricultural Conservation and Natural Resources Policy. 29 pages. Updated February 29, 2016. This report discusses the types and sources of nutrient pollution from agricultural production; possible environmental effects of nutrient pollution; examples of current control measures; the federal response to excess nutrients, including regulatory and incentive-based programs; and future considerations for nutrient management policy at the federal level. Order No. R43919.

PENSIONS

RAILROAD RETIREMENT BOARD: TRUST FUND INVESTMENT PRACTICES, by Scott Szymendera, Analyst in Disability Policy. 10 pages. Updated March 15, 2016. Beginning in 2002, a significant portion of railroad retirement assets have been invested in private stocks, bonds, and other investments. Prior to the Railroad Retirement and Survivors' Improvement Act of 2001, P.L. 107-90, surplus railroad retirement assets could only be invested in U.S. government securities-just as the Social Security trust funds must be invested.3 The 2001 act established the National Railroad Retirement Investment Trust (NRRIT; hereinafter, the Trust) to manage and invest assets in the Railroad Retirement Account in the same way that the assets of private-sector retirement plans are invested. The Railroad Retirement Account is used to fund RRB tier II benefits and supplemental annuities. This account is also used to pay for tier I benefits that are higher than equivalent Social Security benefits, such as early retirement benefits for railroad employees with at least 30 years of railroad service. Assets in the Social Security Equivalent Benefits Account, which is used for RRB tier I benefits that are equivalent to Social Security benefits, continue to be invested solely in U.S. government bonds, as required by law. Bills: H.R. 1140. Order No. RS22782.

PRESIDENTS

FORMER PRESIDENTS: PENSIONS, OFFICE ALLOWANCES, AND OTHER FEDERAL BENEFITS, by Wendy Ginsberg, Analyst in American National Government; Daniel J. Richardson, Research Assistant. 27 pages. Updated March 16, 2016. This report provides a legislative and cultural history of the Former Presidents Act. It details the benefits provided to former Presidents and their costs. Congress has the authority to reduce, increase, or maintain the pension and benefits provided to former Presidents of the United States. This report considers the potential effects of maintaining the FPA or amending the FPA in ways that might reduce or otherwise modify a former President's benefits. Bills: H.R. 1777, S. 1411. Order No. RL34631.

PUBLIC CONTRACTS

MULTIYEAR PROCUREMENT (MYP) AND BLOCK BUY CONTRACTING IN DEFENSE

ACQUISITION: BACKGROUND AND ISSUES FOR CONGRESS, by Ronald O'Rourke, Specialist in Naval Affairs; Moshe Schwartz, Specialist in Defense Acquisition. 19 pages. Updated March 23, 2016. This report provides background information and issues for Congress on multiyear procurement (MYP) and block buy contracting (BBC), which are special contracting mechanisms that Congress permits the Department of Defense (DOD) to use for a limited number of defense acquisition programs. Compared to the standard or default approach of annual contracting, MYP and BBC have the potential for reducing weapon procurement costs by several percent. Potential issues for Congress concerning MYP and BBC include whether to use MYP and BBC in the future more frequently, less frequently, or about as frequently as they are currently used; and whether to create a permanent statute to govern the use of BBC, analogous to the permanent statute (10 U.S.C. 2306b) that governs the use of MYP. Congress's decisions on these issues could affect defense acquisition practices, defense funding requirements, and the defense industrial base. Bills: S. 815, S. 1587, H.R. 4986, H.R. 4739, H.R. 1119, H.R. 1735, S. 1376, S. 3254, H.R. 1960, H.R. 2685, S. 1558, H.R. 2029. Order No. R41909.

PUBLIC LANDS

NATIONAL PARK SYSTEM: UNITS MANAGED THROUGH PARTNERSHIPS by Laura B. Comay Analyst in Natural Resources Policy. 16 pages. Updated April 5, 2016. This report responds to ongoing congressional interest in partnership parks, as Congress seeks to leverage limited financial resources for park management, to respond to concerns about federal land acquisition, and to create park units in ¡§lived-in¡¨ landscapes, where natural and historical attractions are mixed with homes and businesses. It discusses several types of partnership parks:
  -parks with a federal partner;
  -parks with a tribal partner;
  -parks with a state or local government partner;
  -parks with a private partner; and
  -parks with a mix of landowners and management partners.
Bills: H.R. 2636, H.R. 1545, H.R. 2578, H.R. 3820, H.R. 4230, S. 849, S. 2386 Order No. R42125.

REGULATORY REFORM

UNFUNDED MANDATES REFORM ACT: HISTORY, IMPACT, AND ISSUES, by Robert Jay Dilger, Senior Specialist in American National Government; Richard S. Beth, Specialist on Congress and the Legislative Process. 55 pages. Updated March 24, 2016. This report examines debates over what constitutes an unfunded federal mandate and UMRA's implementation. It focuses on UMRA's requirement that CBO issue written cost estimate statements for federal mandates in legislation, its procedures for raising points of order in the House and Senate concerning unfunded federal mandates in legislation, and its requirement that federal agencies prepare written cost estimate statements for federal mandates in rules. It also assesses UMRA's impact on federal mandates and arguments concerning UMRA's future, focusing on UMRA's definitions, exclusions, and exceptions that currently exempt many federal actions with potentially significant financial impacts on nonfederal entities. An examination of the rise of unfunded federal mandates as a national issue and a summary of UMRA's legislative history are provided in Appendix A. Citations to UMRA points of order raised in the House and Senate are provided in Appendix B. Bills: H.R. 50, H.R. 4078, H.R. 899, H.R. 4, S. 189. Order No. R40957.

RELIGION

NONPROFIT CHALLENGES TO THE CONTRACEPTIVE COVERAGE REQUIREMENT: THE MEANING OF

SUBSTANTIAL BURDENS ON RELIGIOUS EXERCISE UNDER THE RELIGIOUS FREEDOM RESTORATION ACT, by Cynthia Brown, Legislative Attorney. 21 pages. March 21, 2016. This report examines the current parameters on governmental restrictions on religious exercise. It discusses the history of federal protection offered under the Free Exercise Clause of the First Amendment and RFRA, and notes parallel protections available at the state level. It analyzes the current interpretations of RFRA as applied to the contraceptive coverage requirement of the ACA, including discussion of Hobby Lobby and a review of the lower courts' interpretations of the nonprofit challenges. Finally, the report highlights a range of issue areas of interest to Congress that may be affected by the Court's interpretation of RFRA. Order No. R44422.

RURAL AFFAIRS

RURAL WATER SUPPLY AND SEWER SYSTEMS: BACKGROUND INFORMATION, by Claudia Copeland, Specialist in Resources and Environmental Policy.
10 pages. Updated February 29, 2016 The Safe Drinking Water Act and the Clean Water Act impose requirements regarding drinking water quality and wastewater treatment in rural areas. Approximately 27% of the U.S. population lives in areas defined by the Census Bureau as rural. Many rural communities need to complete water and waste disposal projects to improve the public health and environmental conditions of their citizens. Funding needs are high (more than $88 billion, according to state surveys). Several federal programs assist rural communities in meeting these requirements. In dollar terms, the largest are administered by the Environmental Protection Agency, but they do not focus solely on rural areas. The Department of Agriculture's grant and loan programs support significant financial activity and are directed solely at rural areas. Meeting infrastructure funding needs of

rural areas efficiently and effectively is likely to remain an issue of considerable congressional interest. Order No. 98-64.

SCIENCE POLICY

NASA APPROPRIATIONS AND AUTHORIZATIONS: A FACT SHEET, by Daniel Morgan, Specialist in Science and Technology Policy. 5 pages. Updated March 11, 2016. In the current fiscal environment, congressional deliberations about the National Aeronautics and Space Administration (NASA) often focus on the availability of funding. This fact sheet provides data on past and current NASA appropriations as well as proposed NASA appropriations for FY2016 and proposed authorizations of NASA appropriations for FY2016. NASA issues of congressional interest are discussed further in CRS Report R43144, NASA: Issues for Authorization, Appropriations, and Oversight in the 114th Congress. Additional information on appropriations legislation affecting NASA is provided in CRS Report R43918, Overview of FY2016 Appropriations for Commerce, Justice, Science, and Related Agencies (CJS), by Nathan James, and similar reports for other years. Bills: H.R. 2578, H.R. 2039. Order No. R43419.

THE INTERNET OF THINGS: CRS EXPERTS, by Eric A. Fischer, Senior Specialist in Science and Technology; Glenn J. McLoughlin, Section Research Manager. 4 pages. Updated March 4, 2016. The table below provides names and contact information for CRS experts on issues before Congress related to the Internet of Things (IoT)-networks of objects that communicate with other objects and with computers through the Internet. "Things" may be virtually any object for which remote communication, data collection, or control might be useful. The full extent of the IoT's impacts is uncertain, but analysts predict contributions to economic growth of trillions of dollars over the next decade. Sectors that may be particularly affected include agriculture, energy, government, healthcare, manufacturing, and transportation. The IoT can contribute to more integrated and functional infrastructure, such as through "smart" electric grids and "smart" cities. Issues that might affect development and implementation of the IoT include economic policy, Internet policy, legal matters, privacy, radio spectrum management, security, technical standards, and the roles of federal agencies. No single federal agency has overall responsibility for the IoT. Various agencies have regulatory, sector-specific, and other mission-related responsibilities, and each agency is responsible for the functioning and security of its own IoT. See also CRS Report R44227, The Internet of Things: Frequently Asked Questions, by Eric A. Fischer; CRS Report R42619, Cybersecurity: CRS Experts; and CRS Report R43382, Data Security and Credit Card Thefts: CRS Experts. Order No. R44225.

SOCIAL SECURITY

RAILROAD RETIREMENT BOARD: TRUST FUND INVESTMENT PRACTICES, by Scott Szymendera, Analyst in Disability Policy. 10 pages. Updated March 15, 2016. Beginning in 2002, a significant portion of railroad retirement assets have been invested in private stocks, bonds, and other investments. Prior to the Railroad Retirement and Survivors' Improvement Act of 2001, P.L. 107-90, surplus railroad retirement assets could only be invested in U.S. government securities-just as the Social Security trust funds must be invested.3 The 2001 act established the National Railroad Retirement Investment Trust (NRRIT; hereinafter, the Trust) to manage and invest assets in the Railroad Retirement Account in the same way that the assets of private-sector retirement plans are invested. The Railroad Retirement Account is used to fund RRB tier II benefits and supplemental annuities. This account is also used to pay for tier I benefits that are higher than equivalent Social Security benefits, such as early retirement benefits for railroad employees with at

least 30 years of railroad service. Assets in the Social Security Equivalent Benefits Account, which is used for RRB tier I benefits that are equivalent to Social Security benefits, continue to be invested solely in U.S. government bonds, as required by law. Bills: H.R. 1140. Order No. RS22782.

SOCIAL SERVICES

CHILD WELFARE: AN OVERVIEW OF FEDERAL PROGRAMS AND THEIR CURRENT FUNDING, by Emilie Stoltzfus, Specialist in Social Policy. 44 pages. Updated March 1, 2016. This report begins with a review of federal appropriations activity in FY2016 as it relates to child welfare programs, including the effect of the automatic spending cuts, known as sequestration. The bulk of the report provides a short description of each federal child welfare program, including its purpose and recent (FY2012-FY2016) funding levels. Bills: H.R. 2029, S. 1799, S. 1695. Order No. R43458.

STATE AND LOCAL GOVERNMENT

UNFUNDED MANDATES REFORM ACT: HISTORY, IMPACT, AND ISSUES, by Robert Jay Dilger, Senior Specialist in American National Government; Richard S. Beth, Specialist on Congress and the Legislative Process. 55 pages. Updated March 24, 2016. This report examines debates over what constitutes an unfunded federal mandate and UMRA's implementation. It focuses on UMRA's requirement that CBO issue written cost estimate statements for federal mandates in legislation, its procedures for raising points of order in the House and Senate concerning unfunded federal mandates in legislation, and its requirement that federal agencies prepare written cost estimate statements for federal mandates in rules. It also assesses UMRA's impact on federal mandates and arguments concerning UMRA's future, focusing on UMRA's definitions, exclusions, and exceptions that currently exempt many federal actions with potentially significant financial impacts on nonfederal entities. An examination of the rise of unfunded federal mandates as a national issue and a summary of UMRA's legislative history are provided in Appendix A. Citations to UMRA points of order raised in the House and Senate are provided in Appendix B. Bills: H.R. 50, H.R. 4078, H.R. 899, H.R. 4, S. 189. Order No. R40957.

WATER INFRASTRUCTURE FINANCING: HISTORY OF EPA APPROPRIATIONS, by Claudia Copeland, Specialist in Resources and Environmental Policy. 37 pages. Updated February 29, 2016. The principal federal program to aid municipal wastewater treatment plant construction is authorized in the Clean Water Act (CWA). Established as a grant program in 1972, it now capitalizes state loan programs. Authorizations since 1972 have totaled $65 billion, while appropriations have totaled nearly $90 billion. It has represented 25%-30% of total funds appropriated to the Environmental Protection Agency (EPA) in recent years.

In appropriations legislation, funding for EPA wastewater assistance is contained in the measure providing funds for the Department of the Interior, Environment, and Related Agencies, which includes EPA. Within the portion of that bill which funds EPA, wastewater treatment assistance is specified in an account now called State and Tribal Assistance Grants (STAG). Three trends in the funding of this account are most prominent: inclusion of non-infrastructure environmental grants to states, beginning in FY1993; increasing number and amount of special purpose grants since FY1989; and the addition of grant assistance for drinking water treatment projects in FY1997. This report summarizes, in chronological order, congressional activity to fund items in this account since 1987. Bills: H.R. 4624, H.R. 3666, H.R. 2158, H.R. 2684, H.R. 2099, H.R. 3019, H.R. 4194, S. 2168, S. 1034, S. 1216 Order No. 96-647.

TAXATION

EXCISE TAX ON HIGH-COST EMPLOYER-SPONSORED HEALTH COVERAGE: IN BRIEF, by Annie L. Mach, Analyst in Health Care Financing. 11 pages. Updated March 24, 2016. The Patient Protection and Affordable Care Act (ACA; P.L. 111-148, as amended) includes a 40% excise tax on employer-sponsored health coverage. This tax, often called the Cadillac tax, is to be implemented beginning in 2018. The excise tax was included in the ACA to raise revenue to offset the cost of other ACA provisions. According to the Congressional Budget Office and the Joint Committee on Taxation, the excise tax is expected to increase federal revenues by $87 billion between 2016 and 2025. The excise tax applies to the aggregate cost of an employee's applicable coverage that exceeds a dollar limit. Applicable coverage includes, but is not limited to, the employer's and the employee's contribution to health insurance premiums and certain contributions to tax-advantaged health accounts (e.g., health care flexible spending accounts, or FSAs). Order No. R44147.

INDIVIDUAL TAXPAYER IDENTIFICATION NUMBER (ITIN) FILERS AND THE CHILD TAX CREDIT: OVERVIEW AND LEGISLATION, by Margot L. Crandall-Hollick, Analyst in Public Finance; Molly F. Sherlock, Coordinator of Division Research and Specialist. 8 pages. March 22, 2016. The child tax credit was created by the Taxpayer Relief Act of 1997 (P.L. 105-34) to help ease the financial burden on families when they have children. The credit offsets a taxpayer's federal income tax liability. It also includes a refundable portion, known as the additional child tax credit (ACTC). The ACTC is available to taxpayers with little or no federal income tax liability. Bills: H.R. 192, H.R. 713, H.R. 1332, H.R. 1333, H.R. 2334, H.R. 2956, H.R. 4722, S. 53, S. 18, S. 1869. Order No. R44420.

TAX REFORM IN THE 114TH CONGRESS: AN OVERVIEW OF PROPOSALS, by Molly F. Sherlock, Coordinator of Division Research and Specialist. 4 pages. Updated March 18, 2016. On December 10, 2014, the Chairman of the House Committee on Ways and Means introduced a comprehensive tax reform proposal, the Tax Reform Act of 2014 (H.R. 1). The bill proposed substantial changes to both the individual and corporate income tax systems, reducing statutory tax rates for many taxpayers, while repealing dozens of credits, deductions, and other tax preferences. While no further action was taken on H.R. 1 in the 113th Congress, the proposal continues to inform the ongoing tax reform debate. Bills: H.R. 1, H.R. 25, H.R. 1040, H.R. 1824, H.R. 25, S. 155, S. 929. Order No. R43060

TECHNOLOGY

FINANCIAL SERVICES AND CYBERSECURITY: THE FEDERAL ROLE, by N. Eric Weiss, Specialist in Financial Economics. 32 pages. March 23, 2016. This report provides information on the landscape of federal laws and regulatory agencies directly regulating or establishing standards for financial services cybersecurity.3 Because each of the applicable federal laws contains specific implementation provisions, there are varying degrees and methods of regulatory oversight of cybersecurity in the financial sector. Some laws distribute authority to issue regulations and take enforcement actions among a number of agencies; others require one agency to issue implementing regulations and distribute enforcement authority among several agencies; and finally, some laws delegate all authority for issuing regulations and administrative enforcement to a single agency. Order No. R44429.

THE FUTURE OF INTERNET GOVERNANCE: SHOULD THE UNITED STATES RELINQUISH ITS AUTHORITY OVER ICANN?, by Lennard G. Kruger, Specialist in Science and Technology Policy. 23 pages. Updated March 22, 2016. Currently, the U.S. government retains limited authority over the Internet's domain name system, primarily through the Internet Assigned Numbers Authority (IANA) functions contract between the National Telecommunications and Information Administration (NTIA) and the Internet Corporation for Assigned Names and Numbers (ICANN). By virtue of the IANA functions contract, the NTIA exerts a legacy authority and stewardship over ICANN, and arguably has more influence over ICANN and the domain name system (DNS) than other national governments. On March 14, 2014, NTIA announced the intention to transition its stewardship role and procedural authority over key Internet domain name functions to the global Internet multistakeholder community. To accomplish this transition, NTIA has asked ICANN to convene interested global Internet stakeholders to develop a transition proposal. NTIA has stated that it will not accept any transition proposal that would replace the NTIA role with a government-led or an intergovernmental organization solution. Internet stakeholders are engaged in a process to develop a transition proposal. While the IANA functions contract was due to expire on September 30, 2015, NTIA has the flexibility to extend the contract for any period through September 2019. NTIA expects that it will receive a final transition proposal in January 2016 with additional time necessary for review, testing, and implementation. On August 17, 2015, NTIA announced that the IANA contract will be extended for one year until September 30, 2016. Bills: H.R. 805, H.R. 4342, H.R. 4660, S. 1551. Order No. R44022.

CYBERSECURITY: CRITICAL INFRASTRUCTURE AUTHORITATIVE REPORTS AND RESOURCES, by Rita Tehan, Information Research Specialist. 31 pages. March 8, 2016

This report serves as a starting point for congressional staff assigned to cover cybersecurity issues as they relate to critical infrastructure. Much is written about protecting U.S. critical infrastructure, and this CRS report directs the reader to authoritative sources that address many of the most prominent issues. The annotated descriptions of these sources are listed in reverse chronological order with an emphasis on material published in the past several years. The report includes resources and studies from government agencies (federal, state, local, and international), think tanks, academic institutions, news organizations, and other sources. Order No. R44410.

ENCRYPTION: SELECTED LEGAL ISSUES, by Richard M. Thompson II, Legislative Attorney; Chris Jaikaran, Analyst in Cybersecurity Policy. 32 pages. March 3, 2016. This report first provides background to the ongoing encryption debate, including a primer on encryption basics and an overview of Apple, Google, and Facebook's new encryption policies. Next, it will provide an overview of the Fifth Amendment right to be free from self-incrimination; survey the limited case law concerning the compelled disclosure of encrypted data; and apply this case law to help determine if and when the government may require such disclosures. The next section of the report will provide background on the All Writs Act; explore both Supreme Court and lower court case law, including a discussion of United States v. New York Tel. Co.; and apply this case law to the San Bernardino case and potential future requests by the government to access a locked device. Bills: H.R. 726, H.R. 2233, H.R. 4651, S. 135, S. 2604. Order No. R44407.

NASA APPROPRIATIONS AND AUTHORIZATIONS: A FACT SHEET, by Daniel Morgan, Specialist in Science and Technology Policy. 5 pages. Updated March 11, 2016. In the current fiscal environment, congressional deliberations about the National Aeronautics and Space Administration (NASA) often focus on the availability of funding. This fact sheet provides data on past and current NASA appropriations as well as proposed NASA appropriations for FY2016 and proposed authorizations of NASA appropriations for FY2016. NASA issues of congressional interest are discussed further in CRS Report R43144, NASA: Issues for Authorization, Appropriations, and Oversight in the 114th Congress. Additional information on appropriations legislation affecting NASA is provided in CRS Report R43918, Overview of FY2016 Appropriations for Commerce, Justice, Science, and Related Agencies (CJS), by Nathan James, and similar reports for other years. Bills: H.R. 2578, H.R. 2039. Order No. R43419.

THE INTERNET OF THINGS: CRS EXPERTS, by Eric A. Fischer, Senior Specialist in Science and Technology; Glenn J. McLoughlin, Section Research Manager. 4 pages. Updated March 4, 2016. A table provides names and contact information for CRS experts on issues before Congress related to the Internet of Things (IoT)-networks of objects that communicate with other objects and with computers through the Internet. "Things" may be virtually any object for which remote communication, data collection, or control might be useful. The full extent of the IoT's impacts is uncertain, but analysts predict contributions to economic growth of trillions of dollars over the next decade. Sectors that may be particularly affected include agriculture, energy, government, healthcare, manufacturing, and transportation. The IoT can contribute to more integrated and functional infrastructure, such as through "smart" electric grids and "smart" cities. Issues that might affect development and implementation of the IoT include economic policy, Internet policy, legal matters, privacy, radio spectrum management, security, technical standards, and the roles of federal agencies. No single federal agency has overall responsibility for the IoT. Various agencies have regulatory, sector-specific, and other mission-related responsibilities, and each agency is responsible for the functioning and security of its own IoT. See also CRS Report R44227, The Internet of Things: Frequently Asked Questions, by Eric A. Fischer; CRS Report R42619, Cybersecurity: CRS Experts; and CRS Report R43382, Data Security and Credit Card Thefts: CRS Experts. Order No. R44225.

TELECOMMUNICATIONS

INTERNET GOVERNANCE AND THE DOMAIN NAME SYSTEM: ISSUES FOR CONGRESS, by Lennard G. Kruger, Specialist in Science and Technology Policy. 33 pages. Updated March 23, 2016. The Internet is often described as a "network of networks" because it is not a single physical entity, but hundreds of thousands of interconnected networks linking hundreds of millions of computers around the world. As such, the Internet is international, decentralized, and comprised of networks and infrastructure largely owned and operated by private sector entities. As the Internet grows and becomes more pervasive in all aspects of modern society, the question of how it should be governed becomes more pressing. Currently, an important aspect of the Internet is governed by a private sector, international organization called the Internet Corporation for Assigned Names and Numbers (ICANN), which manages and oversees some of the critical technical underpinnings of the Internet such as the domain name system and Internet Protocol (IP) addressing. ICANN makes its policy decisions using a multistakeholder model of governance, in which a "bottom-up" collaborative process is open to all constituencies of Internet stakeholders. Bills: H.R. 805, H.R. 805, H.R. 2578, S. 1551. Order No. R42351.

THE FUTURE OF INTERNET GOVERNANCE: SHOULD THE UNITED STATES RELINQUISH ITS AUTHORITY OVER ICANN? by Lennard G. Kruger, Specialist in Science and Technology Policy. 23 pages. Updated March 22, 2016. Currently, the U.S. government retains limited authority over the Internet's domain name system, primarily through the Internet Assigned Numbers Authority (IANA) functions contract between the National Telecommunications and Information Administration (NTIA) and the Internet Corporation for Assigned Names and Numbers (ICANN). By virtue of the IANA functions contract, the NTIA exerts a legacy authority and stewardship over ICANN, and arguably has more influence over ICANN and the domain name system (DNS) than other national governments.

On March 14, 2014, NTIA announced the intention to transition its stewardship role and procedural authority over key Internet domain name functions to the global Internet multistakeholder community. To accomplish this transition, NTIA has asked ICANN to convene interested global Internet stakeholders to develop a transition proposal. NTIA has stated that it will not accept any transition proposal that would replace the NTIA role with a government-led or an intergovernmental organization solution. Internet stakeholders are engaged in a process to develop a transition proposal. While the IANA functions contract was due to expire on September 30, 2015, NTIA has the flexibility to extend the contract for any period through September 2019. NTIA expects that it will receive a final transition proposal in January 2016 with additional time necessary for review, testing, and implementation. On August 17, 2015, NTIA announced that the IANA contract will be extended for one year until September 30, 2016. Bills: H.R. 805, H.R. 4342, H.R. 4660, S. 1551. Order No. R44022

THE CORPORATION FOR PUBLIC BROADCASTING: FEDERAL FUNDING AND ISSUES, by Glenn J. McLoughlin, Section Research Manager; Rita Tehan, Information Research Specialist. 12 pages. Updated March 8, 2016. The Corporation for Public Broadcasting (CPB) receives virtually all of its funding through federal appropriations; overall, about 15% of public television and 10% of radio broadcasting funding comes from the federal appropriations that CPB distributes. CPB's appropriation is allocated through a distribution formula established in its authorizing legislation and has historically received two-year advanced appropriations. Congressional policy makers are increasingly interested in the federal role in supporting CPB due to concerns over the federal debt, the role of the federal government funding for public radio and television, and whether public broadcasting provides a balanced and nuanced approach to covering news of national interest. It is also important to note that many congressional policy makers defend the federal role of funding public broadcasting. They contend that it provides news and information to large segments of the population that seek to understand complex policy issues in depth, and in particular for children's television broadcasting, has a significant and positive impact on early learning and education for children. Order No. RS22168.

TERRORISM

FINANCIAL SERVICES AND CYBERSECURITY: THE FEDERAL ROLE, by N. Eric Weiss, Specialist in Financial Economics. 32 pages. March 23, 2016. This report provides information on the landscape of federal laws and regulatory agencies directly regulating or establishing standards for financial services cybersecurity.3 Because each of the applicable federal laws contains specific implementation provisions, there are varying degrees and methods of regulatory oversight of cybersecurity in the financial sector. Some laws distribute authority to issue regulations and take enforcement actions among a number of agencies; others require one agency to issue implementing regulations and distribute enforcement authority among several agencies; and finally, some laws delegate all authority for issuing regulations and administrative enforcement to a single agency. Order No. R44429.

NAVY IRREGULAR WARFARE AND COUNTERTERRORISM OPERATIONS: BACKGROUND AND ISSUES FOR CONGRESS, by Ronald O'Rourke, Specialist in Naval Affairs. 41 pages. Updated March 25, 2016. This report provides background information and potential issues for Congress on the Navy's irregular warfare (IW) and counterterrorism (CT) operations. The Navy's IW and CT activities pose a number of potential oversight issues for Congress, including how much emphasis to place on IW and CT activities in future Navy budgets. Congress's decisions regarding Navy IW and CT operations can affect Navy operations and funding requirements, and the implementation of the nation's overall IW and CT strategies. Order No. RS22373.

U.S.-EU COOPERATION AGAINST TERRORISM, by Kristin Archick, Specialist in European Affairs. 35 pages. Updated March 2, 2016. Congressional decisions related to data privacy, intelligence-gathering, border controls, visa policy, and transport security may affect how future U.S.-EU counterterrorism cooperation evolves. EU officials have welcomed passage of the Judicial Redress Act (P.L. 114-126) to provide EU citizens with a limited right of judicial redress for privacy violations in a law enforcement context, but they have expressed unease with some provisions in the Visa Waiver Program Improvement and Terrorist Travel Prevention Act of 2015 (passed as part of P.L. 114-113 in the wake of the Paris attacks and heightened U.S. concerns about European citizens fighting with terrorist groups abroad). Given the European Parliament's growing influence in many of these policy areas, Members of Congress may be able to help shape the Parliament's views and responses through ongoing contacts and the existing Transatlantic Legislators' Dialogue (TLD). This report examines the evolution of U.S.-EU counterterrorism cooperation, current issues, and the ongoing challenges that may be of interest in the 114th Congress. Also see CRS

Report R44003, European Fighters in Syria and Iraq: Assessments, Responses, and Issues for the United States, coordinated by Kristin Archick. Bills: H.R. 1428, 4830, S. 1600. Order No. RS22030

TRADE

COUNTRY-OF-ORIGIN LABELING FOR FOODS AND THE WTO TRADE DISPUTE ON MEAT LABELING, by Joel L. Greene, Analyst in Agricultural Policy. 62 pages. Updated March 8, 2016. Since the final rule to implement country-of-origin labeling (COOL) took effect in March 2009, most retail food stores have been required to inform consumers about the country of origin of fresh fruits and vegetables, fish, shellfish, peanuts, pecans, macadamia nuts, ginseng, and ground and muscle cuts of beef, pork, lamb, chicken, and goat. The rules are required by the 2002 farm bill (P.L. 107-171) as amended by the 2008 farm bill (P.L. 110-246). Other U.S. laws have required such labeling, but only for imported food products already pre-packaged for consumers. Canada and Mexico challenged U.S. COOL in the World Trade Organization (WTO), arguing that COOL has a trade-distorting impact by reducing the value and number of cattle and hogs shipped to the U.S. market, thus violating WTO trade commitments. In November 2011, the WTO dispute settlement (DS) panel found that COOL treats imported livestock less favorably than U.S. livestock, and does not meet its objective to provide complete information to consumers on the origin of meat products. In March 2012, the United States appealed the WTO ruling. In June 2012 the WTO's Appellate Body (AB) upheld the DS panel's finding that COOL treats imported livestock less favorably than domestic livestock. But the AB reversed the finding that COOL does not fulfill its legitimate objective to provide consumers with information on origin. The United States welcomed the AB's affirmation of the right to adopt labeling requirements to inform consumers on the origin of their meat. Participants in the U.S. livestock sector had mixed reactions, reflecting the ongoing heated debate on COOL. Bills: P.L. 107-171, P.L. 110-246, H.R. 2393, S. 1844, H.R. 22, P.L. 109-97, P.L. 113-235, H.R. 2642. Order No. RS22955.

FOREIGN CORRUPT PRACTICES ACT (FCPA): CONGRESSIONAL INTEREST AND EXECUTIVE ENFORCEMENT, by Michael V. Seitzinger, Legislative Attorney. 11 pages. Updated March 15, 2016. During the mid-1970s investigations and administrative and legal actions against numerous domestic corporations revealed that the practice of making questionable or illegal payments by United States corporations to foreign government officials existed to some extent within the American business community.1 The legal and regulatory mechanisms for dealing with these payments had involved actions by the Securities and Exchange Commission (SEC) against public corporations for concealing from required public disclosure substantial payments made by the firm, including to foreign government officials. There was also the potential for an antitrust action for restraints of trade or fraud prosecutions by the Department of Justice (DOJ). Government officials and administrators contended that more direct prohibitions on foreign bribery and more detailed requirements concerning corporate recordkeeping and accountability were needed to deal effectively with the problem. The revelations of slush funds and secret payments by American corporations were stated to have affected adversely American foreign policy, damaged abroad the image of American democracy, and impaired public confidence in the financial integrity of American corporations. Bills: H.R. 616, H.R. 5366, H.R. 5837, H.R. 2152, H.R. 3531, H.R. 3588, H.R. 4178. Order No. R41466.

INTERNATIONAL TRADE AND FINANCE: KEY POLICY ISSUES FOR THE 114TH CONGRESS, by Mary A. Irace, Coordinator Section Research Manager; Brock R. Williams, Coordinator Analyst in International Trade and Finance. 38 pages. Updated February 29, 2016

Congress is in a unique position to address these issues, particularly given its constitutional authority for legislating and overseeing international trade and financial policy. This report provides a brief overview of some of the trade and finance issues that may come before the second session of the 114th Congress. Appendix A provides a list of CRS products covering these issues in greater detail. Bills: H.R. 1191, H.R. 2297, H.R. 757, H.R. 3662, H.R. 644, S. 284, S. 433. Order No. R43841.

TRADE PROMOTION AUTHORITY AND THE U.S.-SOUTH KOREA FREE TRADE AGREEMENT, by Robert S. Kirk, Specialist in Transportation Policy. 14 pages. Updated March 17, 2016. Since the beginning of the 112th Congress, convened in January 2011, the House and Senate have observed a ban on earmarks, formally known as congressionally directed spending. The ban has led to changes in the way transportation funding decisions are made. This report explains what earmarks are and discusses their use in surface transportation finance. It then discusses how federal transportation funding is distributed with a ban in place and how Members of Congress might influence the distribution. Order No. R41544.

TRANSATLANTIC TRADE AND INVESTMENT PARTNERSHIP (TTIP) NEGOTIATIONS, by Shayerah Ilias Akhtar, Specialist in International Trade and Finance; Vivian C. Jones, Specialist in International Trade and Finance. 61 pages. Updated February 29, 2016. This report provides: (1) context for the T-TIP negotiations; (2) analysis of possible trade and investment issues in the negotiations; and (3) discussion of issues for Congress. The U.S.-EU negotiations on T-TIP are not public. The information and analysis in this report on issues in the negotiations are based on publicly available information. Bills: H.R. 644. Order No. R43387.

ARGENTINA: BACKGROUND AND U.S. RELATIONS, by Mark P. Sullivan, Specialist in Latin American Affairs; Rebecca M. Nelson, Specialist in International Trade and Finance. 25 pages. Updated March 22, 2016. Argentina, a South American country with a population of almost 42 million, has had a vibrant democratic tradition since its military relinquished power in 1983. Current President Cristina Fernández de Kirchner, from a center-left faction of the Peronist party, the Front for Victory (FPV), was first elected in 2007 (succeeding her husband, Néstor Kirchner, who served one term) and is now in the final months of her second term. Argentina's constitution does not allow for more than two successive terms, so President Fernández is ineligible to run in the next presidential election, with a first round scheduled for October 25, 2015. Eleven candidates competed in an August 9, 2015, combined open primary for electoral alliances, and three top candidates emerged: Daniel Scioli, governor of Buenos Aires province under the banner of President Fernández's FPV; Mauricio Macri, mayor of Buenos Aires, heading the Let's Change coalition that includes center-right and center-left opposition parties; and Sergio Massa, a deputy in Argentina's Congress, who heads a centrist dissident Peronist faction known as United for a New Alternative. This report provides background on the political and economic situation in Argentina and U.S.-Argentine relations. This report provides background on the political and economic situation in Argentina and U.S.-Argentine relations. An Appendix provides links to selected U.S. government reports on Argentina. Bills: H.R. 3049, S.1800. Order No. R43816.

U.S. TRADE CONCEPTS, PERFORMANCE, AND POLICY: FREQUENTLY ASKED QUESTIONS, by Wayne M. Morrison, Specialist in Asian Trade and Finance; Mary Jane Bolle, Specialist in International Trade and Finance; James K. Jackson, Specialist in International Trade and Finance; Vivian C. Jones, Specialist in International Trade and Finance; 48 pages. Updated March 25, 2016. This report provides information and context for these and many other trade topics. It is intended to assist Members and staff who may be new to trade issues. The report is divided into four sections in a question-and-answer format: trade concepts; U.S. trade performance; formulation of U.S. trade policy; and trade and investment issues. Additional suggested readings are provided in an appendix. The first section, "Trade Concepts" deals with why countries trade, the consequences of trade expansion, and the relationship between globalization and trade. Key questions address the benefits of specialization in production and trade, efforts by governments to influence a country's comparative advantage, how trade expansion can be costly and disruptive to workers in some industries, and some unique characteristics of trade between developed countries. The second section, "U.S. Trade Performance," lists data on U.S. trade flows and focuses on the U.S. trade deficit, including its implications for the U.S. economy. Questions address the causes of trade deficits, the role of foreign trade barriers, and how the trade deficit might be reduced. The third section, "Formulation of U.S. Trade Policy," deals with the roles played by the executive branch, Congress, the private sector, and the judiciary in the formulation of U.S. trade policy. Information on how trade policy functions are organized in Congress and the executive branch, as well as the respective roles of individual Members and the President, is provided. The roles of the private sector and the judiciary are also discussed. The fourth section, "U.S. Trade and Investment Policy Issues," lists questions related to trade negotiations and agreements and to imports, exports, and investments. The justification, types, and consequences of trade liberalization agreements, along with the role of the WTO, are treated in this section. The costs and benefits of imports, exports, and investments are also discussed, including how the government deals with disruption and injury to workers and companies caused by imports and its efforts to both restrict and promote exports. The motivations and consequences of foreign direct investment flows are also discussed. Bills: H.R. 1314, H.R. 2146, H.R. 1295. Order No. RL33944

WHAT'S THE DIFFERENCE? -- COMPARING U.S. AND CHINESE TRADE DATA, by Michael F. Martin, Specialist in Asian Affairs. 11 pages. Updated March 24, 2016. There is a large and growing difference between the official trade statistics released by the United States and the People's Republic of China. According to the United States, the 2015 bilateral trade deficit with China was $367.6 billion. According to China, its trade surplus with the United States was $260.9 billion-a $106.6 billion difference. Order No. RS22640.

TRANSPORTATION

FINANCING AIRPORT IMPROVEMENTS, by Rachel Y. Tang, Analyst in Transportation and Industry; Robert S. Kirk, Specialist in Transportation Policy. 30 pages. Updated March 24, 2016. There are five major sources of airport capital development funding: the federal Airport Improvement Program (AIP); local passenger facility charges (PFCs) imposed pursuant to federal law; tax-exempt bonds; state and local grants; and airport operating revenue from tenant lease and other revenue generating activities such as landing fees. Federal involvement is most consequential in AIP, PFCs, and tax-exempt financing. This report provides an overview of airport improvement financing, with emphasis on AIP and the related passenger facility charges. It also discusses some ongoing airport issues that are likely to be included in a future FAA reauthorization debate. Bills: H.R. 4721. Order No. R43327

TRANSPORTATION SPENDING UNDER AN EARMARK BAN, by Robert S. Kirk and William J. Mallett, Specialists in Transportation Policy; David Randall Peterman, Analyst in Transportation Policy. 14 pages. March 17, 2016. Proposals in both the House and the Senate to ban earmarks may lead to changes in the way transportation funding decisions are made. This report explains what earmarks are and discusses their use in surface transportation finance. It then considers how federal highway, transit, and aviation funding might be distributed if such a ban goes into effect, and how members of Congress might influence the distribution. Order No. R41554.

VETERANS

MILITARY FUNERAL HONORS FOR VETERANS, by Scott D. Szymendera, Analyst in Disability Policy. 11 pages. March 23, 2016. Eligible veterans are entitled to receive certain military honors at their funerals. In general, these honors are provided by the Department of Defense (DOD) to eligible veterans who are interred or inurned at Department of Veterans Affairs (VA) national cemeteries, state veterans cemeteries, and private cemeteries. There is no cost to the family of a veteran for military honors. Order No. R44426.

EXPEDITED REMOVAL AUTHORITY FOR VA SENIOR EXECUTIVES (38 U.S.C. § 713): SELECTED LEGAL ISSUES, by Thomas J. Nicola, Legislative Attorney. 22 pages. Updated March 4, 2016. This report discusses selected legal issues relating to the authority for summary removal of individuals in senior executive positions at the Department of Veterans Affairs. Section 707 of the Veterans Access, Choice, and Accountability Act, P.L. 113-146, enacted on August 7, 2014, created this authority by adding Section 713 to Title 38 of the United States Code. It authorizes the Secretary of Veterans Affairs to remove an individual in a senior executive position from federal service or transfer him or her to a position in the General Schedule if the Secretary determines that the individual's performance or misconduct warrants removal. This report addresses whether this authority raises a constitutional question under the Due Process Clause of the Fifth Amendment as a deprivation of a property right to continued federal

employment and whether a court would have jurisdiction to hear a case brought by a senior executive who had been removed pursuant to it. Bills: H.R. 3230, H.R. 4031, H.R. 1994, S. 1082, S. 1117. Order No. R44161.

HEALTH CARE FOR DEPENDENTS AND SURVIVORS OF VETERANS, by Sidath Viranga Panangala, Specialist in Veterans Policy. 18 pages. Updated March 3, 2016. The Civilian Health and Medical Program of the Department of Veterans Affairs (CHAMPVA) was established by the Veterans Health Care Expansion Act of 1973 (P.L. 93-82). CHAMPVA is primarily a health insurance program where certain eligible dependents and survivors of veterans receive care from private sector health care providers. Bills: H.R. 9048, H.R. 5136, H.R. 6523, H.R. 115, H.R. 288, H.R. 218, S. 490, S. 325, S. 170. Order No. RS22483.

VETERANS' BENEFITS: BURIAL BENEFITS AND NATIONAL CEMETERIES, by Barbara Salazar, Torreon Analyst in Defense Budget and Military Manpower. 22 pages. Updated March 11, 2016. This report provides a descriptive analysis of both nonmonetary and monetary burial benefits and national cemeteries. It addresses congressional and constituent issues, such as who is eligible to receive burial benefits; who can be buried in a national cemetery; what plans does the VA have to build new or expand existing national cemeteries; and what benefits does the VA provide, among others. These issues may be of particular interest to Congress due to the aging of the veteran population, the changes to eligibility requirements, and recent VA report findings and recommendations related to the establishment of national cemeteries. Order No. R41386.

WATER RESOURCES

ENERGY AND WATER DEVELOPMENT APPROPRIATIONS FOR DEFENSE NUCLEAR NONPROLIFERATION: IN

BRIEF, by Mary Beth D. Nikitin, Specialist in Nonproliferation. 7 pages. March 8, 2016. The Defense Nuclear Nonproliferation (DNN) programs were reorganized for the FY2016 request. There are now two main mission areas under the DNN appropriation: the Defense Nuclear Nonproliferation Program and the Nuclear Counterterrorism and Incident Response Program (NCTIR). NCTIR was previously funded under Weapons Activities. According to the FY2016 budget justification, "These transfers align all NNSA funding to prevent, counter, and respond to nuclear proliferation and terrorism in one appropriation." Order No. R44413.

WATER INFRASTRUCTURE FINANCING: HISTORY OF EPA APPROPRIATIONS, by Claudia Copeland, Specialist in Resources and Environmental Policy. 37 pages. Updated February 29, 2016. The principal federal program to aid municipal wastewater treatment plant construction is authorized in the Clean Water Act (CWA). Established as a grant program in 1972, it now capitalizes state loan programs. Authorizations since 1972 have totaled $65 billion, while appropriations have totaled nearly $90 billion. It has represented 25%-30% of total funds appropriated to the Environmental Protection Agency (EPA) in recent years. In appropriations legislation, funding for EPA wastewater assistance is contained in the measure providing funds for the Department of the Interior, Environment, and Related Agencies, which includes EPA. Within the portion of that bill which funds EPA, wastewater treatment assistance is specified in an account now called State and Tribal Assistance Grants (STAG). Three trends in the funding of this account are most prominent: inclusion of non-infrastructure environmental grants to states, beginning in FY1993; increasing number and amount of special purpose grants since FY1989; and the addition of grant assistance for drinking water treatment projects in FY1997. This report summarizes, in chronological order, congressional activity to fund items in this account since 1987. Bills: H.R. 4624, H.R. 3666, H.R. 2158, H.R. 2684, H.R. 2099, H.R.

3019, H.R. 4194, S. 2168, S. 1034, S. 1216. Order No. 96-647.

WELFARE

CHILD WELFARE: AN OVERVIEW OF FEDERAL PROGRAMS AND THEIR CURRENT FUNDING, by Emilie Stoltzfus, Specialist in Social Policy. 44 pages. Updated March 1, 2016. This report begins with a review of federal appropriations activity in FY2016 as it relates to child welfare programs, including the effect of the automatic spending cuts, known as sequestration. The bulk of the report provides a short description of each federal child welfare program, including its purpose and recent (FY2012-FY2016) funding levels. Bills: H.R. 2029, S. 1799, S. 1695. Order No. R43458

SECTION 202 AND OTHER HUD RENTAL HOUSING PROGRAMS FOR LOW-INCOME ELDERLY RESIDENTS, by Libby Perl, Specialist in Housing Policy. 30 pages. Updated March 7, 2016. This report provides a summary of the HUD programs that provide multi-family rental housing for low-income elderly households and their related supportive services programs. It also discusses funding and current issues in the area of assisted housing for low-income elderly persons. However, the report does not include a comprehensive look at all housing programs that serve elderly households. Major sources of assistance that are not discussed include HUD's Section 8 voucher program,7 HUD's mortgage insurance and reverse mortgage programs,8 and the Department of Agriculture's rural housing programs that provide assistance to elderly households. Bills: H.R. 8, H.R. 5, H.R. 3, H.R. 31, S. 566. Order No. RL33508.

SECTION 811 AND OTHER HUD HOUSING PROGRAMS FOR PERSONS WITH DISABILITIES, by Libby Perl, Specialist in Housing Policy. 36 pages. Updated March 7, 2016. This report describes how federal funds are used to develop housing designated for persons with disabilities. It also discusses recent funding for the

Section 811 program and current issues surrounding housing for persons with disabilities, including mixed financing arrangements, worst case housing needs, and persons with disabilities who are homeless. Bills: H.R. 12433, H.R. 4, H.R. 5576, H.R. 1158, S. 3084. Order No. RL34728.

THE TEMPORARY ASSISTANCE FOR NEEDY FAMILIES (TANF) BLOCK GRANT: RESPONSES TO FREQUENTLY ASKED QUESTIONS, by Gene Falk, Specialist in Social Policy. 44 pages. Updated March 18, 2016. The Temporary Assistance for Needy Families (TANF) block grant funds a wide range of benefits and services for low-income families with children. TANF was created in the 1996 welfare reform law (P.L. 104-193). This report responds to some frequently asked questions about TANF; it does not describe TANF rules (see, instead, CRS In Focus IF10036, The Temporary Assistance for Needy Families (TANF) Block Grant, by Gene Falk). Bills: H.R. 2029. Order No. RL32760.

WOMEN'S ISSUES

NONPROFIT CHALLENGES TO THE CONTRACEPTIVE COVERAGE REQUIREMENT: THE MEANING OF SUBSTANTIAL BURDENS ON RELIGIOUS EXERCISE UNDER THE RELIGIOUS FREEDOM RESTORATION ACT, by Cynthia Brown, Legislative Attorney. 21 pages. March 21, 2016. This report examines the current parameters on governmental restrictions on religious exercise. It discusses the history of federal protection offered under the Free Exercise Clause of the First Amendment and RFRA, and notes parallel protections available at the state level. It analyzes the current interpretations of RFRA as applied to the contraceptive coverage requirement of the ACA, including discussion of Hobby Lobby and a review of the lower courts' interpretations of the nonprofit challenges. Finally, the report highlights a range of issue areas of interest to Congress that may be affected by the Court's interpretation of RFRA. Order No. R44422.

When you subscribe you will receive;

- Each monthly issue of *Congressional Research Report*,
- Summaries of each week's CRS research output by accessing our *Weekly Report of CRS Documents*,
- Discounted pricing for each report ordered @$7.95 vs. reports starting at $19.95 each.

For an investment of $395 per year.

We have been collecting ALL CRS research documents for the past 23 years.

For a FREE CRS report:

Visit www.PennyHill.com and pick a report from our collection of 70,000+ CRS documents.

Email us the report # at Books@PennyHill.com. It will be delivered to you by email (pdf).